JUDGING PRO BOXING

JUDGING PRO BOXING

Inside the Science, Strategy, & Controversy of Fight Scoring

TOM SCHRECK

THE SECOND BURNING

Copyright © 2026 by Tom Schreck

Cover design by Pixelstudio

Published by Gloves Off Publishing

All rights reserved.

This book reflects the author's opinions and is for informational purposes only. Any activities or exercises are undertaken at your own risk. While advice and strategies may have been effective for some, they may not suit every situation. The author, publisher, and affiliates assume no responsibility for injury, loss, or damages—physical, psychological, emotional, financial, or otherwise. You alone are responsible for your choices, actions, and results.

Library of Congress Control Number: 2026907885
Paperback ISBN: 978-1-971208-24-4
Digital Book ISBN: 978-1-971208-25-1

PRINTED IN THE USA

Contents

Introduction

THE HARDEST SEAT IN THE HOUSE

If you've ever watched a close fight and thought, *"What were the judges watching?"*—you're not alone.

I've heard it in arenas, in bars, on social media, and sometimes shouted directly in my direction from three rows back. In boxing, judging is both essential and perpetually misunderstood. Fighters put their lives into the ring and fans are passionate. Commentators speak with confidence and yet the person holding the scorecard often remains a mystery, or worse, a target.

I've spent three decades in that seat.

Over the years, I've judged professional bouts ranging from small club shows to major cards, to fights-of-the year and I've learned something that may surprise you: most controversies in boxing don't come from incompetence or corruption. They come from misunderstanding, misunderstanding of the scoring criteria, of what judges are trained to look for, and of how difficult it is to evaluate a fight in real time from ringside.

This book grew out of a series of columns I wrote analyzing the craft and science of judging professional boxing. The response to those pieces told me something important. There is a genuine appetite from fans, fighters, trainers, and even media to better understand how fights are actually scored.

What you'll find in these pages is not a defense of bad judging because bad judging exists. Poor scorecards happen because judges are human, and like anyone working under pressure in real time, they can make mistakes.

But what you will also find is that many decisions labeled "robberies" are anything but. Close rounds are often exactly that—close. Reasonable, well-trained judges can and do disagree, especially in fights where styles clash and momentum shifts subtly from minute to minute.

Judging professional boxing is one of the few jobs in sports where every decision must be made in real time, without replay, from a fixed angle, while the crowd reacts emotionally and while the fighters themselves are constantly adjusting

There is no pause button at ringside.

In the chapters that follow, I'll walk you through the fundamentals of the 10-point must system, the four official scoring criteria, and the subtle elements, the educated jab, the effective aggressor, the quiet defensive move, that often separate winning rounds from losing ones. We'll also examine where statistics like CompuBox help and where they mislead, why media scorecards often diverge from official ones, and why the word *robbery* is probably the most overused term in the sport.

Most importantly, I'll try to bring you into the judge's chair.

Because once you understand what trained officials are actually looking for, and what they are not, the sport begins to look different, cleaner, and more nuanced. Sometimes it becomes more frustrating, but almost always more interesting.

Boxing doesn't need fewer opinions. It needs better-informed ones.

If this book helps you watch the next close fight with a sharper eye and a little more appreciation for the difficulty of the task, then it will have done its job.

Let's take a seat at ringside.

Tom Schreck

ONE

How Scoring Evolved Into The Ten Point Must System

IF YOU'VE WATCHED a fight in the last fifty years, you've heard it announced: "All three judges score the bout 115–113..."

Those numbers, so familiar they're practically part of boxing's DNA, come from the Ten-Point Must System—the method that defines modern professional scoring. But where did it come from? And why ten points? To understand that, you have to go back to when judging was simpler, rougher, and far more subjective.

WHEN THE REFEREE WAS THE ONLY JUDGE

For much of boxing's early history, there were no ringside judges at all. The referee alone decided who won the fight. He was part cop, part mediator, and part arbiter. That made sense in an era when most bouts ended in knockouts.

But when fights went the distance, chaos followed. Referees had to make a single, sweeping decision with a winner or loser without a structured scoring system. Fans and managers cried foul, newspapers split their verdicts, and hometown bias was rampant.

By the 1910s and '20s, as the sport professionalized and money poured in, commissions began experimenting with systems to bring some order to the chaos.

THE "ROUNDS WON" ERA

The first serious attempt at structure was the Rounds Won System, used widely in the 1920s and '30s. Under this model, each round was treated like a miniature contest: the fighter who performed better in that round was awarded the round, and whoever won the *most rounds overall* won the fight.

A ten-round fight, for example, might end with one boxer taking six rounds, the other four. The scores would be announced as "six rounds to four" rather than numerically.

HOW IT WORKED

- Judges (and often the referee) marked a tally each round for the fighter they thought won.
- "Even" rounds were common when the action was too close to call.
- At the end of the bout, the fighter with the most rounds won took the decision.

THE LOGIC BEHIND IT

The "Rounds Won" system appealed to regulators because it was simple and mimicked baseball's "inning-by-inning" logic: whoever wins the most segments wins the game.

It also mirrored the common-sense idea that a fighter who wins six rounds out of ten *should* win the fight, even if he got hurt late.

Its Strengths

- Clarity: Fans could understand it instantly.

- Fairness over the long haul: Rewarded consistent control rather than late rallies.
- Ease of training: Judges didn't need to learn point arithmetic.

Its Weaknesses

- No degree of dominance. A fighter who barely edged a round got the same credit as one who dominated it.
- Too many "even" rounds. Judges often called close rounds even, leading to drawn fights that satisfied no one.
- No cumulative punishment. A fighter could lose six rounds narrowly but win four by huge margins—and still lose the fight.

By the 1930s, reformers wanted something that would *quantify dominance* without overwhelming judges with math. The answer came from New York.

THE FIVE-POINT MUST SYSTEM

Before the Ten-Point era, the Five-Point Must System was implemented in the 1940s. It governed hundreds of world-title bouts and set the foundation for what followed.

HOW IT WORKED

- Each round began with both fighters theoretically even at five points.
- The *winner* of the round must receive five points.

- The *loser* received fewer, depending on how decisively he lost.
    - Close round → 5-4
    - Clear loss → 5-3 or 5-2
    - Near-knockout → 5-1
- Fouls directed by the referee resulted in a further point deduction.

A typical ten-round card might look like this:

Round	Fighter A	Fighter B
1	5	4
2	5	4
3	4	5
4	3	5
5	5	4
6	5	4
7	4	5
8	5	3
9	5	4
10	5	4
Total	**46**	**42**

ROUND: FIGHTER A

Fighter A wins 46–42. The spread reflected both who won and how clearly he won each round.

THE LOGIC BEHIND IT

The Five-Point system kept the round-by-round accountability of "Rounds Won" but introduced degrees of margin.

Judges could express whether a round was close or dominant, something the earlier system couldn't handle.

Its Strengths

- Required decisiveness. The "must" rule forced judges to pick a winner each round.
- Added nuance. A 5–4 wasn't the same as a 5–2.
- Controlled subjectivity. A small, five-step scale kept scores tidy and limited wide discrepancies.

Its Weaknesses

- Too compressed. Judges couldn't show subtle differences between rounds.
- Unintuitive totals. Scores like 48–45 confused fans and promoters.
- No national consistency. Other commissions used different methods.
- Television optics. Broadcasters found the numbers awkward to explain on air.

TRANSITION TOWARD TEN

By the 1960s, several commissions—including Nevada—were testing a Ten-Point Must model that simply doubled the five-point range.

- Judges now had ten integers instead of five, giving finer gradation.
- Totals like 115–113 looked cleaner and more intuitive.
- When the World Boxing Council (WBC) formally endorsed the Ten-Point system in 1968, the Five-Point approach quickly faded, though its DNA lives on every time a 10–9 round is read aloud.

THE BIRTH OF THE TEN-POINT MUST SYSTEM

The modern system took shape in the United States in the mid-20th century. The Nevada State Athletic Commission is widely credited with first experimenting with a ten-point variant as early as the 1940s, seeking a more flexible and transparent scale.

Two decades later, the WBC formally adopted and promoted it worldwide, cementing it as boxing's universal standard.

The goals were clear:

1. Consistency. Each round starts at ten; the winner must receive ten, the loser less.
2. Clarity. Totals like 115–113 convey competitiveness at a glance.

3. Flexibility. Knockdowns or dominance can
    widen the spread to 10–8, 10–7, or beyond.

WHY TEN?

Ten wasn't mystical—it was practical.

Five points didn't offer enough distinction; twenty was too cumbersome. Ten hit the sweet spot: simple, scalable, and easy for fighters, fans, and judges to grasp.

The "Must" in the System

That single word—*must*—was revolutionary. One fighter must receive ten points except in a rare 10–10 round.

The intent was to end indecision: every round had to have a winner. It forced accountability and gave the sport a consistent rhythm of judgment.

WHY SO MANY 10-9 ROUNDS?

Though the system allows 10–8, 10–7, or 10–6, most rounds are scored 10–9.

- Competitiveness: Few rounds are dominant
  enough to justify two-point margins.
- Training discipline: Commissions teach restraint
  —reserve 10–8 for clear control or knockdowns.
- Human psychology: Judges avoid "over-
  punishing" for brief lapses.

The result: fights cluster around 115–113 or 116–112, showing close competition more than one-sided beatings.

ALTERNATIVES AND ADJUSTMENTS

Experiments have come and gone—half-points (10–9.5), open scoring, computerized tallies—but none replaced the Ten-Point Must.

Recent reforms from the Association of Boxing Commissions (ABC) urge judges to use 10–8 rounds without knockdowns when dominance is obvious. It's a sensible evolution that stays true to the system's spirit.

The System's Strength—and Its Flaw

Its strength is its universality: a 10–8 round means the same in New York, Tokyo, or Las Vegas.

Its flaw is human: interpretation will always vary.

For all its imperfections, the Ten-Point Must remains the sport's best balance between structure and subjectivity.

It compels decisiveness while preserving the artistry of judgment—a fitting reflection of boxing itself.

Sidebar: The Evolution of Scoring Systems in Boxing

Era / System	How It Worked	Strengths	Weaknesses
Referee-Only (pre-1920s)	Referee alone decided the winner after the final bell.	Simple and decisive.	Highly subjective; hometown bias.
Rounds-Won (1920s–1930s)	Judges tallied rounds won; majority of rounds determined the fight.	Easy to understand; rewarded consistency.	No scale for dominance; too many "even" rounds.
Five-Point Must (New York 1940s–60s)	Round winner got 5; loser 4 or fewer.	Introduced "must" rule; added nuance.	Narrow range; confusing totals; inconsistent nationally.
Ten-Point Must (Nevada 1940s → WBC 1968 – Present)	Winner *must* get 10; loser ≤ 9.	Flexible, intuitive, global standard.	Overreliance on 10–9; subjective application.
Half-Point / Experimental (2000s)	Allowed 10–9.5, 10–8.5, etc.	Added nuance.	Confusing and inconsistent.
Computerized Amateur (1990s–2010s)	Judges pressed buttons for clean punches.	Objective in theory.	Ignored ring generalship; abandoned.

TWO

The Scoring Criteria and the Concept of Doing Damage

I'M BETTING you don't need to be told that the four scoring criteria for professional boxing are Clean Punching, Effective Aggressiveness, Ring Generalship, and Defense. In fact, I would bet just about everyone reading that last sentence could hear the beloved Harold Lederman recite them in their head.

The four criteria are supposed to act as a guide for how a round is scored. The problem is defining each one away from the abstract and into something that is objective, consistent among those doing the scoring, and easy to understand. Saying you know it when you see it, like Justice Potter Stewart's statement on pornography, isn't really scientific, nor does it help to make scoring concrete and measurable.

Professional boxing is, at its essence, about doing damage. In today's world, that phrase would not be lauded by the politically correct, and honestly, there is something a bit distasteful about the terminology in a world where CTE robs so many collision sport competitors of their quality of life as they age.

Still, professional boxing is about assessing damage. Let's work that notion into our existing criteria, starting at the bottom and moving to the top.

Defense is, of course, central to competitive boxing. If you're getting hit more often and harder than your opponent, chances are you will not win the round. Legend has it that Willie Pep once told boxing writers that he was going to win a round without throwing a punch and then proceeded to do it, on, I believe, two of the three scorecards. That may or may not be true, but I believe it would be exceedingly hard to win a round by merely employing better defense.

Broken down, this criterion would probably be most accurately described as "defense that leads to clean punching that causes damage." The goal of professional boxing is to strike your opponent, and employing good defense will set you up to do just that. Think of Pernell Whitaker or a young Hector Camacho—both fighters had great defense, but that defense didn't win them rounds if it didn't lead to offense. You can't win at boxing without a solid defense, but you can't win at boxing with only a solid defense.

Ring Generalship may be the hardest criterion to define. It means controlling the ring and the action, and that can take a myriad of forms. It may be who is moving forward more often, but not necessarily; it might mean who is cutting off the ring effectively, but not necessarily; and it might mean who is positioning themselves to be able to score. However, and this is a big however, if that generalship doesn't lead to scoring blows, what does it actually mean? Is your ring generalship worthy of note if it didn't lead to a damaging scoring blow?

Probably not.

Effective Aggression is a criterion that carries a modifier. "Effective" is the key term here. Aggression, in the scoring sense, means getting punches off, pushing the exchanges, engaging in the fight, and physically demonstrating the willingness to box. What is ineffective aggression? You've seen it, and you recognize it, even if in the moment you don't describe it by its official name.

Think of the fighters that chase their opponent around the ring, missing their haymakers and getting tagged by a back-peddling counter puncher. Think of the boxer who huffs and puffs and growls, who gets tied up, spun around, and countered by their opponent. And think of the fighters that throw with damaging intention only to have their shots blocked and countered.

Aggression needs to be effective.

It is effective when it leads to scoring blows, right? Any other type of aggression would be tough to describe as effective, wouldn't it?

Which leads me to the first criterion: Clean Punching. A clean punch is one that lands with proper form and body mechanics with the knuckle part of the boxing glove. Some purists and martial artists might even argue that it should be the first two knuckles of the fist because that would mean that the fist, back of the hand, and arm would all be in alignment. That might be just a tad of minutia, but it helps to conceptualize the proper form of the punch.

There's a reason there are a limited number of punches in the sport. There's the jab, the cross, and the hook, and some derivations like the overhand, the bolo, and others. Since the times of John L. Sullivan, fighters have learned that creating new punches often leads to disastrous results. Power and defense come from body mechanics and proper form, and deviating from that reduces the efficiency of your attack.

There are no doubt obvious exceptions to this. Muhammad Ali kept his hands low and often punched without the weight of his body behind his shots. Roy Jones Jr. did many fundamentally unsound things in the ring but compensated for it with Herculean conditioning and strength.

Exceptions aside, a good clean punch looks like a good clean punch because it comes with the proper form and bodyweight behind it. A boxer's weight should be moving behind the punch for maximum effect, so when you see a boxer throwing but keeping their weight on their back leg, they are executing a punch without maximum efficiency and power.

It is easier and faster to throw punches without the weight of your body behind it. You can also get out of danger faster when your feet aren't firmly planted. Old-timers will tell you that punches come from the ground up and with a strong foundation based in the legs. No one will ever cite Rocky Marciano as the sweetest in this sweet science, but watch him throw his hooks and see the power in his legs.

It is clean, properly executed punches that cause damage. Some boxers bring more power with their body mechanics, and that can be seen in what the punches do to the opponent. Moving a fighter off their stance, snapping their head to the side and back, and buckling their knees are all observable and should be what goes into scoring a round.

So, when you think about it, all the criteria—Effective Aggression, Ring Generalship, and Defense—should result in clean punching. Clean punching leads to damage.

The fighter that does the most damage wins the round.

Just a word or two about my contributions to Boxingscene. I am an active judge, so it won't be appropriate for me to cover current fighters, bouts, officials, commissions, or sanctioning bodies. My articles will be focused on the principle of judging for the most part, and hopefully, they may help readers understand what they are watching better.

And it is totally okay if you've disagreed with my scorecards in the past. You learn to have thick skin in this biz, and I know criticizing the officials is part of sports. Honestly, when I'm watching a game from the last row of the end zone at Notre Dame Stadium, I don't hesitate to yell at the refs 95 **yards** away for missing a holding call.

Future articles will look at the anatomy of controversial decisions, the hardest rounds to score, how TV differs from live fights, analysts and their work, and judging different styles. If you'd like me to cover something in particular, drop me a note.

THREE

The Anatomy of a Controversial Decision

WHY ARE THERE SO many controversial decisions in our sport?

There are a bunch of reasons that I'd like to suggest and outline for you, and you probably have your own list as well. Inherent in all of the reasons is the fact that boxing matches are decided by a scoring criteria that, despite the best efforts of everyone in the sport, remains subjective—that is, it is up for interpretation.

Let's break down how controversy comes about.

First of all, and let me get this out of the way first, sometimes judges blow it.

There, I said it.

Boxing judges, like the rest of us, are flawed human beings. Sometimes even the best judges can have a bad night. The sport tries to mitigate that fact by having three judges. But sometimes even three judges can have a bad night.

Are all judges equal in ability? Probably not, just like surgeons, lawyers, quarterbacks, and plumbers come in all levels of ability. Again, having multiple judges to score a fight is meant to mitigate the danger of having a not-so-accurate score.

Is there corruption in judging? Like, someone with a trench coat and wide-brim fedora shows up with a brown paper bag filled with non-sequential C-notes and says something to the judges like, "Hey kid, it's not your night."

I've been doing this for 27 years, and it has never happened to me, nor have I ever seen it.

That's all I'm going to say about that.

With that out of the way, let's explore how controversial decisions come about or are perceived to come about.

DIFFERENT STYLES

In my previous articles, I've talked about scoring and the hard rounds to score. I won't rehash all of them here except to say that some judges will score one style over another. So, when you're watching a bout between a good jabber and a power fighter, a fight with very little action, a fight with an abundance of action, or a bout with strong ebbs and flows, expect there to be a difference in scoring.

When that preference or interpretation differs from yours—and this is a big *and*—differs from the broadcast crew, many will see the scoring as flawed and in error.

That's when the C-word starts to be bandied about.

I guess what we all hope for is that there is one absolute —and only one absolute—way to score the action. We can hope for that, but it hardly seems realistic. I believe there are going to be rounds that are likely to be interpreted in different ways.

Is that controversial?

Maybe *debatable* would be a better word.

FORGETTING THAT ALL ROUNDS COUNT THE SAME

Those boring opening rounds count the exact same as the exciting championship rounds. When the opening half of a fight has very little action, it is easy to dismiss them and even forget about them entirely. You're on your couch, you're enjoying a beverage, you stop to greet the Grubhub guy—hell, why not? Not much is going on inside the ropes.

Well, those guys in the jackets and ties sitting on the barstools ringside have to turn in a scorecard every single round, whether it was a Hagler-Hearns-type round or something to watch when you're out of melatonin. Those rounds count the same.

10-9 is 10-9, and most rounds are scored 10-9. Maybe that's a flaw in the scoring system, but that *is* the scoring system. If you were in an alley watching a street fight that started slow and then progressed to where one hoodlum was beating the crap out of the other ne'er-do-well, it would be easy to say who won.

Professional boxing isn't in an alley and it isn't a street fight.

I know I've said it, but I'll say it again:

All the rounds count the same.

FORGETTING THAT BOXING IS A SPORT

Look, I'm a believer in the adage, *"You don't PLAY boxing."*

This is a brutal sport, and its goal is to do damage. Having said that, it is still a sport with a point system. When your favorite fighter walks in to land his or her power shots and takes a bunch of shots on the way in, you may think, "Wow, what a badass tough son-of-a-bitch!" But you know what? He or she probably just lost the round.

Sugar Ray Leonard, Hector Camacho, and Pernell Whitaker knew how to win rounds. Ray Leonard once said that he didn't have to be angry or hate his opponent—he saw it as a sport. He was a great champion, and he understood the scoring system. You may or may not have liked the style of *The Macho Man*, especially later in his career, but he scored points and got out of the way—a perfect formula for winning rounds.

Elite fighters know how to win rounds. They score punches that are easy to see, they know when to pick up the action, and they avoid punishment. Boxers who let themselves get hit and smile while waving their opponent back in aren't racking up the points. In a gym session, everyone watching might think that guy is toying with his opponent, doing whatever he wants and having his way. That may be the case, but that's not how points are scored. It may make you the coolest guy at the Saturday afternoon sparring session, but it won't win you rounds.

Busy fighters—even when they're less skilled and less powerful than their opponents—can take rounds by just doing more. When they do that against a bigger name or fighter with the rep, some might see a controversy.

Score the round as you see it.

That's all.

THE NON-CLOSE SCORE IN A CLOSE FIGHT

Championship fights are actually 12 separate three-minute fights. Judges are supposed to forget about the rounds that came before the current round and not daydream about the rounds that are coming.

Some rounds can be razor-thin close.

Sometimes all 12 rounds can be razor-thin close.

Sometimes a fighter does just a fraction more to tilt the judges' decision.

The judges will even tell you after the fight that it was razor-thin close.

So… it is possible that a razor-thin, super-close fight could end up 120-108, couldn't it?

Yes.

Each round was super close, but one fighter did just a little more each round. It ends up in a perfectly justifiable one-sided score that will undoubtedly lead to controversy.

Announcers, writers, message board contributors, and fans won't see it that way. They will argue that it was way too close to have a score that wide. The fact is that it definitely could come out that way. Fights are scored round by round.

And when scores come in like 116-112, 116-112, 117-111, or even 118-110, you do realize that over 12 rounds, in a close fight, all of those scores could be considered on target? When you analyze the master scoring sheet, you can see that the totals can be different, but if judges were in agreement over most of the rounds, is that really appalling? With the three-judge system, the judge with the differing score could even have been in agreement with at least one other judge in every round.

Their total comes out different, but it doesn't mean they had an off night.

TELEVISION ANNOUNCERS, COMPUBOX, SLOW-MOTION REPLAY

TV wants to put on a good show. One of the things I do outside of boxing is write mystery novels and plays. Any writing instructor will tell you that conflict is essential to tell a good story. Developing a storyline that a decision is fraught with controversy makes things interesting, doesn't it?

If, when they announce the decision, the TV guys said something like, "Yeah, I can see that—that seems about right," wouldn't that feel out of place?

If you've been to a TV fight and you look at the announcers, you can see they're as busy as a one-legged man in an ass-kicking contest. They're listening to the booth, heading to the corners between rounds, setting up promos, and the crew is tapping them on the shoulder—it is relentless.

Some TV folks seem to score really well, but not all of them. Viewers tend to believe what they hear. It is entertainment when you're on the couch. When you're judging, you are trying to see everything, concentrate on it, and evaluate it in the moment. You have no outside data, no differing opinion, and no analysis except your own. It is not the same thing as taking in a fight for enjoyment.

People ask me all the time how I scored a fight I watched on TV. Usually, I say I watched it but I didn't score. I know the difference.

If you want to score at home, you absolutely must turn off the sound, ignore CompuBox numbers, and don't watch the replays or the TV judge's score. It affects you even when you think it doesn't. To score a fight like a real judge, view it as much as you can like a real judge.

Watching fights like that isn't fun, but you may get to a score that differs with TV.

You may even agree with some of the "controversial" scoring.

Wouldn't that be interesting?

FOUR

But How Do You Really Score a Round?

"HOW DO YOU SCORE A ROUND?"

Easily the question I get asked the most.

And—not so coincidentally—the one I talk about the most in this column. Up until now, I've bored you with the scoring criteria, the concept of doing damage, the misconceptions of scoring, and other chestnuts that I'm sure you and your boxing fans talk about endlessly.

Yeah, right.

What smart fans *really* want to know is: how the hell do judges come up with the scores they do?

Like everything else in life, there's a process. There's an actual way of doing it. Scoring a round isn't just about memorizing the criteria—it's an active, second-by-second mental engagement. There's theory, and then there's application.

You want a surgeon who not only knows anatomy but knows how to cut you open, move stuff around, and take out the bad parts. There's knowledge, and then there's practiced skill. You want that from your surgeon—and you should want that from your boxing judges.

Boxing is scored by observing what's right in front of you as two fighters do their thing. Sometimes they're doing things simultaneously, and a judge has to decide what's more effective. Scoring starts at the sound of the bell and evolves in real time. A judge keeps an internal score running as the round unfolds.

The internal dialogue might sound like this:

Hagler moves forward and throws... Leonard slips and blocks... score stays even.

Leonard misses with a pawing jab... Hagler lands two solid body shots... Hagler leads 10-9.

Leonard moves... Hagler misses... Leonard plants and fires a three-punch combo, most of it blocked... round tightens, but Hagler still ahead 10-9...

The Association of Boxing Commissions uses four terms to describe how clearly a fighter is winning a round:

- **Close** – a narrow margin
- **Moderate** – clearly in favor of one fighter
- **Decisive** – one fighter is clearly imposing their will and doing damage

There is even an **Excessive Decisive** round, which refers to a clearly dominant round and usually warrants a **10-8** score. Knockdowns almost always get an additional point.

But here's where nuance comes in.

If Fighter A is winning a round in decisive or excessive decisive fashion but then suffers a knockdown, that doesn't automatically make it a 10-8 for Fighter B. That might still be a **10-9** round—judges are supposed to weigh the overall effectiveness and flow of the round, not just one moment.

To give you a feel for how this internal process plays out, I've applied mine to Round 10 of Hagler vs. Leonard. It's a tight round that demands focused attention.

Watch it. Then listen in on my mental scoring process. https://youtu.be/SGiubSEqy38

What you'll notice (besides the fact that I probably don't have a future in play-by-play) is:

1. The judge should be mentally engaged *every second* of the round.
2. A working score should begin early in the round.
3. The score is dynamic—changing based on the degree of action and effectiveness.
4. At any moment, if the round stopped, the judge should be ready to submit a score instantly.

This takes concentration. It's not rocket science, but it's not passive viewing either. You've got to understand what punches are landing, how hard, and how much damage they might be doing.

You can't do it with an IPA in your hand and a basset hound on your lap.

Do all judges follow this mindset every round? No. They're human. They get tired, distracted, and sometimes they lose focus. But they shouldn't.

The goal is simple: be present, watch closely, and score *every second* from bell to bell.

FIVE

The Science of the Jab
& Why It Wins Rounds

IN PROFESSIONAL BOXING, the most important punch is often the least appreciated.

Fans gravitate toward power shots, and broadcasters react to the big heavy cross. Highlight reels are constructed around knockout shots. But round after round, fight after fight, the jab quietly does the work that decides scorecards.

The jab is not just a punch; it is the control system of the fight. When used well, it manages distance, dictates pace, disrupts offense, and racks up clean scoring blows with remarkable efficiency. From a judging standpoint, those qualities matter more than flash.

EFFICIENCY: WHY THE JAB SHOWS UP ALL NIGHT

One reason the jab is so influential is simple physics.

It travels the shortest distance. It requires less weight transfer. It allows the puncher to stay balanced and defensively responsible. Because of that, elite fighters can throw it repeatedly without burning the kind of energy required for hooks and right hands.

Over the course of a 10- or 12-round fight, that efficiency adds up. The fighter with the better jab is often the fighter who can maintain steady, effective offense deep into the bout while his opponent begins to slow.

Judges don't score effort directly, but they absolutely see the results of efficient work.

CONTROL OF THE FIGHT

At its core, boxing is about who is forcing the other man to react.

A consistent, accurate jab does exactly that. Every time it lands or threatens to land, the opponent must make a decision: slip, parry, reset his feet, or hesitate before coming forward. That constant disruption adds both physical and mental strain.

Meanwhile, the jabber is operating on his terms.

From ringside, this often shows up as one fighter looking composed and in rhythm while the other looks slightly out of sync. Even in otherwise close rounds, that difference can be meaningful.

SETTING THE DISTANCE AND THE TONE

The jab is also the primary tool for what judges refer to as ring generalship.

A good jab:

- Establishes range
- Keeps the opponent at the end of punches
- Creates safe entry points
- Forces resets
- Allows the puncher to step in behind it

When one fighter is consistently determining where exchanges take place, he is controlling the geography of the fight. Judges are trained to notice this, even when the crowd does not.

You'll often hear fans say a fight is "close," but from the chair, one boxer may clearly be the one setting the terms, usually behind the jab.

NOT ALL JABS ARE EQUAL

This is where experienced judges separate from punch counters.

A meaningful jab is:

- Clean
- Accurate
- Thrown with intent
- Landing without being immediately countered
- Affecting the opponent's position or rhythm

By contrast, pawing, range-finding touches that don't land clean or don't influence the opponent carry far less scoring weight.

Volume matters. But effective volume matters more.

Can You Win a Round Mostly on the Jab? Absolutely.

Consider a typical close round:

- Fighter A lands steady, clean jabs throughout
- Controls distance
- Forces Fighter B to reset repeatedly

Fighter B may land an occasional harder right hand, but if those moments are sporadic while Fighter A is consistently dictating the action, many experienced judges will lean toward Fighter A.

Why? Because the scoring criteria reward:

- Clean punching
- Effective aggression
- Ring generalship
- Defense

A disciplined jab can check all four boxes in a single round.

WHY THE JAB GETS UNDERVALUED

There are a few predictable reasons:

First, visual bias. Power shots are dramatic. Jabs are subtle.

Second, crowd influence. Big punches draw reactions that steady lead hands rarely do.

Third, punch stats. CompuBox tracks jabs and power punches, but it does not measure control, who is forcing resets, who is dictating range, or who is making the other fighter uncomfortable.

Judges are not scoring noise. They are scoring effectiveness.

THE QUIET REALITY OF CLOSE FIGHTS

In many competitive bouts, especially at the higher levels, there are no knockdowns and no overwhelming power disparities. These are the fights where the jab becomes decisive.

When evaluating a tight round, experienced judges often come back to three questions:

- Who controlled the distance?
- Who dictated the pace?
- Who forced the other fighter to react more often?

More often than not, the fighter with the better jab is the one answering those questions.

And when that happens consistently, the scorecards tend to follow.

SIX

Blood and Chins

WHY SOME FIGHTERS LOOK WORSE BUT WIN

You SEE a fighter bleeding from a cut over the eye and think, "He's losing." The other guy is fresh-faced and composed. Easy round to score, right?

Not so fast.

In professional boxing, judges aren't scoring how *hurt* a fighter looks. They're scoring *what caused the visible effects*, and more importantly, how *effective* those punches were in terms of impact and ring control. And here's the tricky part: not all damage is created equal, and not all fighters react to punches the same way.

Some guys swell up like balloons after a jab. Others take flush right hands all night and don't blink. The ability to "take a punch" or not is often baked into a fighter's biology. Call it "chin," "durability," or "punch resistance." Whatever the label, it complicates how judges evaluate fights.

CUTS, BRUISES, AND BLEEDERS

Fighters like Arturo Gatti and Henry Cooper were notorious for cuts. It didn't mean they were losing; just that their facial tissue scarred and split more easily. Some guys bruise from glancing shots. Others get headbutted and look like they went through a windshield. Good corners know to talk to the referees and doctors before fights to make sure those professionals know of a fighter's tendencies when it comes to cuts.

As a judge, you learn to ignore the blood and look at how it got there. Was it one clean uppercut or a series of jabs? Was the cut from a punch or an accidental clash of heads? A cut can end a fight on a TKO, but until that moment, it doesn't necessarily win you rounds.

THE GLASS JAW VS. THE GRANITE CHIN (AND TEX COBB)

Then there's the chin—the legendary but mysterious factor in boxing lore.

Some fighters get touched and their legs betray them. Others absorb bombs and walk through fire. Fans call the first group "glass-jawed" and the second "iron-chinned," but there's real science behind it.

No one embodied the "granite chin" quite like **Randall "Tex" Cobb**, especially in his 1982 heavyweight title fight against Larry Holmes. Holmes landed over **300 clean power punches**, yet Cobb never went down. He took a sustained, almost inhuman beating for 15 rounds and was still smiling through the blood. It was such a display of durability that Howard Cosell reportedly walked away from calling boxing after it aired.

Cobb's performance wasn't about scoring rounds; he lost every one. But it showed that having a good chin isn't about being unhittable; it's about *not folding when hit*. Judges had to score that fight not based on Cobb's toughness, but on Holmes's dominance, even if Cobb looked like he could go another 15.

Neurologically, a punch causes rotational acceleration of

the brain. The force can disrupt the vestibular system—your body's internal balance mechanism. If that disruption reaches a certain threshold, the fighter staggers, drops, or shuts down momentarily. It's not just pain; it's a disconnection of signals.

Some fighters have stronger neck muscles, which help stabilize the head and reduce that whip-like motion. Others may have more fluid in the brain to cushion movement, better recovery times, or just genetic luck. Unfortunately, repeated concussive blows can change that over time. A great chin in your twenties doesn't always stick around.

JUDGING THE IMPACT OF IMPACT

Let's say Fighter A lands a clean counter that visibly wobbles his opponent. Fighter B lands more total punches, but they don't have much effect. If that moment of visible damage outweighs the rest of the round, judges may score it for Fighter A. That one punch *mattered more*—not just because it looked good, but because it altered the round's dynamic.

But what if Fighter B *was* hurt but has a great poker face? What if Fighter A bleeds from the nose and looks worse off, even though he controlled the action?

Judges don't have medical scans. They have human eyes, experience, and the mandate to score *effective aggression*, not *cosmetic damage*. The guy who looks fresh might actually be losing. And the guy bleeding from a cut might be in total control.

FINAL THOUGHTS

Fans love visible drama—blood, knockdowns, legs buckling. But judging a fight is about what landed clean, what had effect, and who imposed their will. Some fighters show damage more. Some take punches better. And some can be stunned by a jab.

There's no simple formula for scoring a round. But when you understand that a bruised face isn't the whole story, and that chin strength is as much science as folklore, you start to see the sweet science in a whole new light.

THE SCIENCE OF THE CHIN

Why some fighters crumble from a jab and others eat right hands for breakfast

- **Neck Strength Matters:** Strong neck and trapezius muscles help reduce the rotational "whiplash" effect from punches. Less head movement equals less brain rattle.
- **Vestibular System Shock:** Getting "buzzed" isn't about pain; it's about a disruption to your inner ear and balance system. That's why wobbly legs can follow even a glancing blow.
- **Cerebrospinal Cushioning:** Some people have more fluid around the brain, acting like natural suspension. More cushion equals less trauma from impact.
- **Genetics and Bone Structure:** Thicker jaws, broader skulls, and deeper-set chins can all help absorb force better. Think Tex Cobb or George Chuvalo.
- **Recovery Rate is Key:** Getting rocked isn't always what loses the round; it's how fast you recover. Some fighters "reset" in seconds. Others never shake it off.

- **Cumulative Damage:**Even the best chins fade. Every shot taken in sparring or under the lights chips away. Today's iron chin can be tomorrow's glass.

SEVEN

The Score Implications of Style

FILM STUDY: "STYLES MAKE FIGHTS."

IT IS one of our sport's most popular clichés. Like most clichés, it takes the place of a thorough explanation and instead provides shorthand to what is a more complex dynamic. Different styles present challenges to judges in that the judges must interpret the action within the scoring framework when what the two boxers are doing may appear quite different.

To illustrate that, I'm going to use as a reference some fighters from the not-too-distant past. Their differences and how they were able to execute can illustrate how their styles affect scoring.

The boxers:

Hector Camacho – Incredible movement and defense, outstanding speed, and remarkable counterpunching. As he moved up in weight, his power was sometimes questioned, as was his tendency to put safety first.

Julio Cesar Chavez—A dominant power fighter who would wade in on his opponent, sometimes taking punches to land his own. He wore opponents down, was very difficult to hurt, and his punches unquestionably did damage.

Tony Baltazar—Fought for the title twice. Waded in with his power and liked to wear his opponents down with volume and power. Could be hit and countered with speed and agility.

Pernell Whitaker—Very hard to hit, even from close in.

Excellent defense but did it, unlike Camacho, without always using his feet. Could counterpunch and land punches in combination, but his power wasn't his strong suit.

Now, class, you have some homework to do. I want you to watch the following bouts (or at least the highlights when the full bouts aren't available):

Camacho vs. Baltazar
Camacho vs. Chavez
Whitaker vs. Chavez

CAMACHO VS. BALTAZAR

**https://www.youtube.com/watch?v=
JZ8t0tl76wg(full fight)**

In the midnineties, when Camacho moved up in weight, he did not bring the power and aggression he showed in his earlier fights at lighter weights. Baltazar was a smart fighter, and his strategy was to crowd Camacho, rough him up, bully him, and wear him down.

Camacho's goal was to hit and not get hit, move and counter.

This wasn't a hard fight to score. Camacho wins this fight easily.

Why? Why could Camacho impose his strategy when Baltazar couldn't?

When Baltazar moved into the neutral zone to throw, Camacho met him with a jab and then got out of the way. Determined, Baltazar continued to try but continued to get hit and fail to score. Over time, the aggressor wants to keep pushing, but as they get countered, they begin to hesitate, which exacerbates the issue. As they hesitate, they are easier to counter, take more punishment, and lose rounds. Camacho could do this with brawlers and did it throughout the nineties successfully. He certainly did it to Baltazar on this night.

But Camacho couldn't always do it, and when he fought the best brawlers with exceptional power, he struggled.

CHAVEZ VS. CAMACHO

https://www.youtube.com/watch?v=-hj1tNw S_X4(highlights)

Chavez simply didn't seem to be bothered by Camacho's jabs and counters. He never hesitated and continued to move forward, almost ignoring Hector's punches. Julio's power negated Camacho's speed and agility. He successfully cut off the ring. The Macho Man couldn't plant his feet to land anything that would slow Julio down, and it was a terrible beating.

Why could Chavez do what Baltazar couldn't?

Power, ability to cut off the ring, and the ability to take a punch. It wasn't that there was merely a style that could beat Camacho; it was the power and the ability to do damage. Simply put, Chavez hurt Camacho too much for Hector to execute what he could do against Tony Baltazar.

CHAVEZ VS. WHITAKER

https://www.youtube.com/watch?v=-NoFi TZIYpA(highlights)

Whitaker and Camacho had somewhat similar styles with a couple of important differences. Whitaker evaded punches but stayed in position to counter. Camacho moved out of danger, which kept him from being a threat to Chavez. Somehow, Sweet Pea also could take Chavez's punishment better than Camacho. Perhaps it was because of the very subtle movement he presented that made it difficult for Julio to land flush. Maybe he landed shots but never the home run because of Whitaker's subtle movement.

The fight ended in a controversial draw, but that doesn't take away what Sweet Pea was able to do during the fight. He landed, he countered, and he didn't get hurt. He stayed in position and was able to gain respect with his punches— all things that Camacho couldn't do.

From a judging perspective, we can assess which fighter in these cases is imposing their will effectively and doing damage. What allows them to do it or not seems to be due to factors like the ability to take a shot, the ability to stay in position to land, and the ability to do damage, whether that is through accumulation (Camacho vs. Baltazar), through power (Chavez vs. Camacho), or the ability to evade and, this is the important part, make the boxer who misses pay with power (Whitaker vs. Chavez).

In pro boxing, it isn't merely landing; it is landing and doing damage. It is why we can't simply say that one style will dominate another. Instead, it is what that style is able to do against that opponent. The brawler won't always beat the flashy boxer or vice versa. The truly great generational fighters bring a variety of tools to the workshop. Ray Robinson could beat you with speed, power, counterpunching, or any number of techniques. There was only Ray Robinson, and there aren't many fighters who can beat you in a variety of ways.

You may be a fan of a particular style, but while assessing performance, you must evaluate the fighter's ability to execute. That means a fighter can win even going backward—when you hate that style. A fighter can win by executing perfect defense and landing very clear counters—

even if you hate that style. Fighters can have an ugly style to watch and may eat punches on the way in, but if they do and then wreak damage, they can win the round—even if you hate that style.

Style may make fights, but it is doing damage that wins fights.

EIGHT

Willie Pep

SCORING THE PUNCH-LESS WINNING ROUND

WILLIE PEP IS my favorite all-time old-school fighter. TwoWith two hundred and twenty-nine wins against 11 losses and one draw, he won and regained the Featherweight title, competed in three decades, and, this is my favorite, defended his title six months after being in a plane crash and having doctors tell him he'd never box again.

His defense and movement were legendary. He carried the nickname "The Will-o'-the-Wisp" because he glided in and out of harm's way in the ring while stopping to counter and do damage. He was beautiful to watch and worth a deep dive into YouTube to gain some appreciation of his mastery.

Like with many bigger-than-life figures, legends surround Pep. Maybe the most enduring legend is that Pep promised writers that he'd win a round without throwing a punch. Before fighting Jackie Graves, a very solid opponent, he supposedly announced in the third round that he'd win while mounting zero offense. It is often reported as truth in documentaries about PepPep, and that he even carried two of the three scorecards in the third that night.

Did it happen?

The answer is a decidedly, probably not.

We know Pep won the fight, but no film of it exists. It was before reporters and filmmakers reported on the official scorecards, so we can't rely on that either. In fact, reporting was so inconsistent in that era that the AP and the UPI disagreed on how many times Graves went down in the fight —one news service said twice, and the other reported four knockdowns.

Pep liked to talk about the round, and it was said that he even carried around an article of the fight that supposedly verified that he won the round without throwing a punch. Some even claimed that Willie wrote the article himself. Late in life, Graves said he didn't remember if he lost the round without Pep throwing a punch but said it was possible because he was that hard to hit.

"I believe he did it. The man was a legend and a star beyond boxing. He hung out with guys like Jackie Gleason and Frank Sinatra—why would he need to make up anything to make himself seem bigger?" James Madio says. Madio starred in *The Featherweight*, the 2024 biopic on Pep. *The New Yorker* said in its Academy Awards issue that Madio should've been nominated for best actor.

Regardless of whether the myth is true, the fact remains that Willie Pep was one of the most elusive boxers to ever step into the ring. His defensive skills were truly something to behold, and you could see his influence on fighters like Ali, Camacho, and Whitaker. His footwork and lateral movement, his feints and misdirection, and his head movement left opponents bewildered and often frozen. He slipped, bobbed, weaved, and parried with ridiculous balance.

Still, can all of that without throwing a punch win you a round?

"Unless the other boxer didn't throw any punches either, you can't win a round without throwing a punch," Joe Cusano says. Cusano is a longtime pro ref and judge, and he made a cameo appearance in the movie playing, of course, a referee. "He would have had to throw something." Cusano's book, *Uppercuts*, will be released later this year.

Could Pep's charisma have helped him to win a punch-less round? One part of the legend is that he told the judges what he was about to do.

"Hey, if Willie leaned over the ropes and talked to the judges, that might've gotten in their heads, and maybe that influenced them," Madio says. It wouldn't be the first or last time that a fighter influenced judges.

To justify scoring a round for a fighter who didn't throw a single punch would involve some pretty abstract thinking. When you apply the four scoring criteria, it would mean there would be no clean punching and zero aggression, let alone effective aggression. I guess you could earn points for defense and ring generalship, but usually, those two supportive criteria count when they lead to clean punching. If a fighter just evades without countering, that's not really worthy of points.

The opponent, as Joe Cusano points out, would have to be complicit in his passivity by missing all of his punches and perhaps not even throwing any. I think if one fighter didn't throw any punches at all and the other boxer threw punches that didn't land, that would probably be enough to give that fighter the round.

"I spent a whole day with Willie at the Hall of Fame, and we talked a lot about this," Mark Baker, Pep's biographer, says. "It always sounded shaky, and the more I prodded, the more the story kind of fell apart. Eventually, Willie said he probably jabbed or threw punches but didn't land."

Jabbing and throwing punches that might not have landed is a whole lot different from not throwing any punches. You could certainly win a round doing those things.

"Willie was quite a character, and he was given a bit to telling tall tales," Baker says. Baker also has some insight into how the article got written and how the legend developed.

"In those days, reporters and writers sent their accounts over the wire. Their accounts of the fights were often quite inaccurate. On the night of the Pep-Graves fight, there was quite a bit of sunspot activity that would have interrupted the transmission. That would have left a lot of holes in the account of the fight. The guy who wrote the article that Willie carried with him was a pretty obscure reporter and may have taken the opportunity to write something sensational."

The Featherweight will have a wide release in May on various streaming outlets. Mark Baker's book *Willie Pep: A Biography of the 20th Century's Greatest Featherweight* is available on Amazon, as will Joe Cusano's forthcoming boxing book *Uppercuts.*

NINE

Scoring from The Judge's Chair vs. Scoring Watching TV

JUDGES OFTEN SAY that fights are much different in person, and that accounts for the differences and controversies in the game. There are some key differences between the live judging experience and watching from home on your 55-inch 4K screen.

That said, I think claiming that fights are totally different on TV can be a cop-out. There are differences, but I'd argue those differences are more nuanced than pronounced.

Let's take a look at the differences:

THE ANGLE

Being close to the best fighters in professional boxing is a privilege. Seeing the finest in the game up close is something I never take for granted. However, the angle of view isn't always ideal for catching all the action, especially when the fighters are across the ring. One fighter might have their back to you, and when the two boxers are primarily infighting, it can be challenging to catch everything.

In these situations, television usually switches to a camera on the ring apron for a better view. I wish judges could get that! When the action is far away and a fighter has their back to you, it can be difficult to evaluate what's happening.

REFEREE INTERFERENCE

Refs have a tough job, and ensuring the safety of the boxers is their top priority, not avoiding obstructing the views of three judges seated around the ring. I would much rather they focus on the boxers' safety, keeping the action legal, and ensuring knockdowns and cuts are correctly noted.

Still, I sometimes find my view obstructed by a referee's position. Television, on the other hand, can easily switch angles to give viewers a better perspective. Some referees even attempt to officiate from the ringside without a judge, pacing only that side of the ring, but that's an awful lot to ask.

You can miss a critical shot because of a referee's positioning—there's just no way around it. Judges might shift in their seats to improve their view, but sometimes it's simply impossible.

COMMENTATORS

Announcers can help viewers keep up with the action when it's fast or hard to follow. They act as another set of eyes, sharing their interpretation of what's happening. Most of them split their attention between the monitor and the ring, juggling multiple demands.

However, viewers are often subject to the commentators' interpretation. If you're watching passively, their opinions may seep into yours unless you actively focus and form your own evaluation.

Judges, on the other hand, don't have monitors or someone whispering in their ear to explain what happened.

EVALUATING POWER

One of the biggest surprises I encountered when I began judging televised bouts was how difficult it is to assess power through the two dimensions of a TV broadcast. Early in my career, I judged a close fight and gave significant credit to a boxer for his bodywork. But when I watched the recording, those punches, which seemed hellacious in person, appeared average on screen. I learned that power isn't always as obvious on TV.

I've had the privilege of judging great body punchers like Miguel Cotto and Triple G. At ringside, their punches looked so devastating I thought, "If I ever took a shot like that, I'd never go to the bathroom right again." On TV, those same punches looked like solid body shots, but their true power wasn't as apparent.

Headshots can be easier to evaluate on TV, as good ones often make the head move. A particularly hard shot might visibly affect the fighter. However, the sheer resilience some fighters display when absorbing those hits is awe-inspiring. Watching live, it's impossible to ignore.

THE ROPES

Every arena has unique stools for us to sit on, and the rings vary in height, which affects how the ropes are positioned. Sometimes, you spend the evening hunched over, peering through the bottom two ropes; other times, you lean back to look through the top two. It's far from ideal.

Some judges stand and move around, but I avoid that. Fans who've paid good money to sit ringside deserve an unobstructed view. Besides, moving around can be its own distraction.

Recently, a broadcast team positioned a camera behind us to show viewers what it's like. Let's just say it didn't become a fan favorite.

DISTRACTIONS

At home, you miss the chaos and excitement that occur live: fights breaking out in the audience, camera operators squeezing past to film a corner between rounds, or ring card girls climbing through the ropes. Depending on your seat, you might even overhear the announcers' commentary.

Harold Lederman, one of the kindest people I've ever met, used to announce his scores loudly every three rounds —it was hard to ignore. Fans can also be quite vocal, cheering wildly for every blow their fighter lands, even when the punch is blocked. The sound of wet leather slapping gloves might excite the crowd, but a blocked shot isn't a scoring blow.

Cornermen are rarely silent. While some keep their shouts to simple encouragement, others seem to use it as a tactic to influence judges. "There you go!" or "He didn't like that!" might be attempts to sway us, but you don't hear it as clearly on TV.

CONCLUSION

All in all, watching on TV is fairly close to the in-person experience—not the same, but close. Some fights are razor-thin in margin, and in these cases, the difference between TV and live viewing might be enough to cause a disparity.

TEN

Mindfulness in the Judge's Chair

JUDGING PROFESSIONAL FIGHTS IS CHALLENGING. The crowd is deafening, the corners are shouting, the announcers are audibly doing their thing, and the fans in the arena are letting their passion be heard. In the middle of all that, judges need to keep their minds steady, their eyes sharp, and their scorecards impartial.

That kind of focus doesn't happen by accident. For many judges, it takes discipline, preparation, and even a few rituals. In recent years, I've found myself thinking more about what you might call mindfulness: the ability to quiet the noise and stay in the moment when the environment is screaming at you to lose focus.

A SPIRITUAL RESET

Before every fight, I say a short silent prayer: *"Please protect the fighters, please let the right boxer win, and please help me score the bout correctly."*

It's spiritual, not doctrinal. It isn't about bringing religion into the ring. It's about centering myself and remembering why I'm there: to safeguard fighters and give them a fair shake.

I once spoke with Las Vegas judge and referee Robert Hoyle, and he told me he says the same exact prayer. Neither of us claims it guarantees a perfect scorecard. What it does is remind us that the night isn't about us. It's about the fighters, their safety, and their work.

THE MANTRA OF STILLNESS

Then, just before the opening bell, I give myself a mantra: *"Be still and be ready."*

Those five words pull me into the moment. They help shut out stray thoughts about the crowd, the corners, or even what I ate for dinner, and prepare me for the rhythm of the fight. A boxing match is chaos. Every round is a storm of sound and movement. A mantra becomes a kind of anchor, keeping your attention where it belongs.

THE PSYCHOLOGY OF DISTRACTION

Why does mindfulness matter in judging? Because distraction is everywhere.

Crowd noise can turn a partially blocked punch into what sounds like a knockout blow. A fighter's reputation can make a jab look sharper than it is. A flurry at the end of a round can feel bigger than steady work throughout. Even something as superficial as flashy trunks or a famous cornerman can tilt perception.

Judges know this, and commissions remind them constantly: score what you see, not what you hear or feel. But awareness alone doesn't make it easy. Mindfulness gives you a process for managing those biases. It helps you reset and come back to the four scoring criteria: clean punches, effective aggression, defense, and ring generalship.

LESSONS FROM OTHER SPORTS

This idea isn't unique to boxing. In figure skating and gymnastics, judges are taught visualization and breathing exercises to help block out crowd influence. In martial arts, referees use brief meditations before bouts. Even in the NBA, referees talk about developing rituals to reset after a bad call or a hostile crowd reaction.

The principle is the same across sports: you can't control the environment, but you can control how you meet it.

PRACTICAL MINDFULNESS FOR JUDGES

Mindfulness doesn't mean detachment. It means being fully present. For judges, that translates to:

- **Reset each round.** Treat every three minutes as a clean slate.
- **Score only what lands.** Not what looks flashy, not what draws cheers.
- **Ignore the noise.** Corners, crowds, reputations, and histories don't land punches.
- **Stay present.** Each exchange is its own moment.

In a 12-round fight, that means making 12 separate mini-verdicts. Each one has to stand on its own. Mindfulness makes that possible.

THE HUMAN FACTOR

At the end of the day, judges are human. No mantra or prayer makes us infallible. But these practices, whether spiritual or mental, are tools that help us do our job under some of the most distracting conditions in sports.

The best judges I know spend as much energy on awareness as they do on anything else. They develop rituals to stay grounded. They remind themselves why they're there. They work on clearing away everything that doesn't belong on the scorecard.

WHY IT MATTERS

When judges lose focus, fighters pay the price. Careers get sidetracked, titles shift unfairly, and fans lose faith in the sport. Bad decisions erode boxing's credibility. Mindfulness isn't a cure-all, but it's a way to give fighters the fairest chance possible.

Because in the end, judging is about more than knowing the rules. It's about knowing yourself and keeping yourself out of the fight.

ELEVEN

Concentration

HOW MINDFULNESS CAN SHARPEN YOUR ATTENTION

"Get your mind in the game!" "Focus, dammit!" "Remember the rulebook!" "No mistakes this time!" "Ignore the crowd!" The hell with the television and the fans!"

If this is the self-talk you employ to get your head in the game, you're doing it wrong. Sure, we're all told to concentrate; in fact, we're told to do that over and over, and that it is THE most important thing we need to do to be a competent official. Often, that message comes from stressed-out supervisors who really want the coaches, media, and fans off their backs.

However, the "Concentrate, dammit!" philosophy isn't the best way to bring about the optimal mental state. Not only is it not the best way to get your head in the game, it is actually the worst. There's a better way to get the focus you want that is not only more efficient but also doesn't involve demanding unrealistic mental states or superhuman senses.

Now, I bet I have your attention.

THE DANGER OF FALSE CONFIDENCE

Whoa, we were talking about concentration, not confidence, weren't we?

Yes, indeed we were, but they are closely aligned. We've

all met the type of official—you know the ones—who don't admit to any nervousness before a game. They say they don't care at all about what's written about them, or care that the fans boo their very existence, or worry that an emoji in their image has been hung in effigy in an internet forum. They play themselves off as superhuman because nothing bothers them. No anxiety and not a hint of self-doubt ever darkens the corners of their consciousness.

Alan Goldberg, one of the nation's top sports performance consultants, has an opinion on such personalities.

"They're denying reality, of course. An individual about to officiate a big game or significant contest will have some anxiety. The deniers believe that admitting such nervousness to themselves or others will cloud their judgment. The reality is that there is a part of their mind that knows they are deluding themselves. When you fight a thought in your mind, like denying nervousness, it just makes that thought stronger," Goldberg said.

Unpleasant emotions like anxiety aren't bad or even undesirable. They are simply part of our experience in life and in officiating. Pretending they are not there or shouting them down internally only makes them come back stronger; that's just how our mind and our internal voices work. It is useless to try to fight it.

"False confidence isn't in the best interest of an official. Let's be honest: if someone says they don't have any nervousness before a significant performance, then they are out of touch. They may pretend that they don't see what they are about to do as a challenge or a threat, which would naturally bring on an emotional reaction," Gary Bennett said. Bennett is a licensed clinical psychologist specializing in sports psychology at Virginia Tech.

Bennett says a good portion of what we think will be negative because that's how the mind has evolved.

"The trick isn't to deny the feelings but to recognize them and reinterpret them. Anxiety can be interpreted as a desire to do well and to really get involved," Bennett said.

So, are we left to just think things are going to go wrong, that we could, and quite possibly will, screw up and must let our minds run all over us?

No, that's not it at all. There's a different path to head down.

"The answer is learning to change your relationship with the self-talk and distractions presented by our minds," Alan Goldberg said.

CHANGING YOUR RELATIONSHIP WITH YOUR THOUGHTS

Never mind the social-worky play on words; the key to effective concentration is getting in touch with how your thoughts come about and how your mind works. I don't know if you've noticed, but your mind doesn't produce a constant stream of positive, life-affirming thoughts. In fact, if we are honest, our minds spit out cognitions that are quite often judgmental, condemning, and negative. Furthermore, our minds remain resistant to our efforts to change these types of thoughts. You can use positive imagery, listen to self-help gurus, and run your old self-hypnosis tapes about manifesting perfection, but when all is said and done, your mind is likely to tell you it is all crap, everyone is crap, and crap is all we ever have to look forward to.

This isn't a mistake. Our species didn't evolve because we were always upbeat, pleasant, and optimistic. No, us Homo sapiens are still around because we were vigilant, obsessed with danger, and given minds that provided us with an endless feedback loop of how things could go wrong. It kept our forefathers a step ahead of saber-toothed tigers, made them study which plants they thought might make a nice salad and which would kill them, and had them preparing to deal with the horrible weather that would eventually come and threaten their safety.

Today, the mind functions the same way, constantly reminding us of threats, real, imagined, and everything in between. So we worry about being late for work, we fret about retirement, and we want to know right away what that mole on our backside means. And if you care about being a competent official and value the sport you oversee, you are concerned about getting your calls right because if you don't, there are consequences. The wrong team could win, or a player might get hurt. If you truly value the game and perform poorly, you may lose the opportunity to remain close to the game, forfeit what peers think of you, and definitely lose the approval of players, their parents, and their fans. In other words, there are important things at stake.

We also evolved to value having others like us, and officiating puts us in a position where some, or even many, people won't like us at all. You can go ahead and pretend that doesn't matter to you, not even a little bit, and that it doesn't ever enter your mind. If that's what you're shooting for or pretending to have already mastered, good luck with that.

"Positive thinking, positive imagery, and things like that might feel good, especially when your event is far away. It is likely that when it gets close, you will have plenty of negative thoughts," Alan Goldberg said. "The problem isn't the thoughts; the problem comes when you engage your thoughts. The answer is learning to change what you focus on."

That change in relationship starts by acknowledging that you have negative thoughts, self-doubts, and anxieties. That mindset takes a self-awareness that you should work on as much as you do the rules of your game. Without self-awareness, you simply won't improve.

"Concentration is having the ability to focus on what's important and let go of everything else," Goldberg said.

That means being aware of the unimportant thoughts and having the presence of mind to still do your job. It is a process that can't be done without thinking, and most of all, thinking about your thoughts. Psychology now sees mindfulness as the key to performance and self-acceptance.

"You can't stop the negative thoughts, but you can choose what to focus on," Gary Bennett said. "Mindfulness is about being able to pay attention to the right thing, being able to focus on what you value, and basing your behavior on those values rather than on thoughts that you don't have complete control over."

HOW TO DO IT: THE RIGHT STATE OF MIND

Your senses involve a complicated process, and in officiating, there are a lot of things coming at you at once. There is the game itself, of course, the reaction of the coaches, the fans, and the players, and there are the stimuli brought on by the arena or stadium, the camera people, and the lights. There are also the stimuli that are going on inside of you, including your thoughts, emotions, and other cognitions. Many times, these internal stimuli take the form of words and sentences that form a narrative in between our ears.

"There are two things you can do. One will cause you to be anxious and preoccupied and have you performing way below your potential," explains Alan Goldberg. "When you focus on your thoughts and your thinking, things like what others think of you, the consequences of making a mistake, and what the future will bring, you are internally focused."

Goldberg says our thoughts and cognitions, the messages we consciously tell ourselves, reside in our front brain. The front brain reacts after self-talk and evaluation. It is slow and inefficient.

The other choice you have, according to Goldberg, is to have an external focus. When you employ this, you are in the moment, seeing and reacting to the environment around you. This is where we perform best because we are reacting to what is in front of us, not what is going on in our heads. We rely on our knowledge and experience, not self-talk.

"When we have an external focus, we shift the work to our hindbrain. This part of the brain is non-judgmental, examines what it senses as a whole, and processes complex stimuli instantaneously. It is where peak performance occurs. While the front brain is processing voices and thoughts, the hindbrain is acting. You want to be in your hindbrain while officiating," Goldberg said.

We can focus on the past, present, or future in our minds. Only the now is real. The past and the future live only in our thoughts. To get into the now, you need to be aware of what is going on in your mind.

HOW TO DO IT.

The way to bring about the optimized mindset is to be mindful. The simplest exercise to bring this about is to focus on your breathing without trying to control it or change it in any way. Just observe the inhales and the exhales. While you're doing this, note what thoughts and emotions come into your consciousness. Observe them in a detached way and do not try to control them. It is important to realize that you are not your thoughts and you have very little, if any, control over what enters your mind. Do not attempt to stop the thoughts or convert them. Instead, watch them with the curiosity of a third-party scientist. When the thoughts are negative or even disturbing, allow them to exist and realize they will either eventually lessen, worsen, or even stay the same, but they do not define you or have to influence anything you do. Decide to exist along with whatever your mind offers you.

This is where you can change your relationship with them. Instead of fighting your thoughts or attempting some sort of mental gymnastics to avoid them, shift your focus to what is really important to you.

"We want to base our behavior on what we value, not the thoughts that we do not have complete control over," Gary Bennett said. "Get in touch with what you really value and make a commitment to act on that rather than your thoughts. It is vital to do this all the time, not just when things are going well."

It takes some introspection to know what you value about your position. If what you really value is ego, attention, and the impression you make on others, you are far more likely to get stuck in the nether regions of your front brain. There, you will remain internally focused and filled with distracting thoughts about whether your performance is good enough, and it will all be to keep up with your ego.

On the other hand, if you value getting the very next call as right as you can in the moment, if you value a fair outcome to the game, and if you value the safety of the athletes, you are more likely to be externally focused. This creates a seeing and reacting mindset where you are in the zone of picking up the stimuli outside of you and reacting with the body of your experience and knowledge behind you. Your super-efficient and fast hind brain will act without you having to filter it through the thought-filled, muddy waters of your front brain.

PRACTICE

Concentration is a skill, and one you can work on with deliberate practice. It is not the same skill as memorizing your rulebook. That is also time well spent, but that is not what we're looking for here. You want to work the mechanism that keeps you in the now, activates your hind brain, and gets you seeing and reacting.

"I worked with some of our athletes at Va Tech by having them listen to the Hallelujah Chorus. First, I had them listen to it without instructions," Gary Bennett said. "But then I had them listen and focus only on the sopranos. Then we went back to the entire song and then on to another part. It helped train them to understand that there are many things going on at once," Bennett said.

Perhaps the simplest form of concentration training is to sit and focus on your breathing. Call it meditation if you like, but while you focus on your inhales and exhales, thoughts and feelings will come to mind. Practice noticing them, labeling them, and making conscious room for them while you gently return your focus to your breathing. It is this exact mechanism that you will employ in officiating when you find yourself in the past or the future and you need to be brought back to the now. The beauty of this exercise is that you can do it all day, anywhere, and for as long as you want. It will open up a world of awareness about what goes on inside of you and how little control you have over it.

It is also important to do some work on what you value. Take pen and paper and write down the kind of official you want to be. Be honest, and when you notice the ego-driven part of you, refocus on the values that are centered on the betterment of the games and your sport as a whole. It is those values you will want to commit yourself to and base your behavior on when your concentration slips.

Mindfulness is a lifelong process that we tend to slip in and out of. Spend some time really taking in where you are in the moment, what is going on with your thoughts, and your physicality. There is more our attention can pick up than that which we are currently aware of.

TWELVE

Judging Two-Minute Rounds

Sɪᴛ ʀɪɴɢsɪᴅᴇ ꜰᴏʀ ᴀ ᴛᴡᴏ-ᴍɪɴᴜᴛᴇ ʀᴏᴜɴᴅ, and you immediately notice the difference. The pace is quicker, the action more compact, and the scoring trickier. For judges, those 120 seconds present a unique challenge.

In a three-minute round, a fight often develops in layers. The first minute may be tentative, with the fighters testing each other. The second minute brings adjustments. It's often in the third minute where separation occurs when one boxer asserts control, lands the telling shots, or forces the other onto the defensive. That third minute is where the story of the round is often written.

In two-minute rounds, you don't get that luxury. The story has to be told in fast bursts, with fewer chances for clear dominance to emerge. As a judge, you're asked to make the same definitive call, but with less material to work with.

THE CLOCK AS A FACTOR

We don't usually think about time itself as a factor in scoring, but it is. A shorter round is naturally more volatile. One clean combination can outweigh a half-dozen jabs if it lands at the right moment. A sharp flurry in the final seconds can sway perception, even if the other fighter was steadier overall.

That's not an excuse for sloppy judging; it's a reminder

that the clock changes how fights are fought and how we evaluate them. In two-minute rounds, every second is magnified.

STAYING SHARP

That magnification means judges can't afford to ease into a round. You have to be focused from the first exchange. There's no room for mental drift and no chance to "wait and see" if a fighter takes control late. The round might already be over.

It also means you can't overvalue a single burst of action. A fighter who throws a fast 10-second flurry shouldn't automatically steal a round if the other fighter controlled the previous 110 seconds. Judges need to train themselves to weigh the full two minutes, not just the last impression.

EXPERIENCE, TECHNIQUE, AND POWER

Two-minute bouts take place in women's boxing. One of the ongoing discussions in the sport is whether women should box three-minute rounds like men. Until that changes, we as judges have to adapt to the format as it is.

It's worth noting that most women's divisions are contested at lighter weights, where fights naturally feature less one-punch knockout power. The same is true on the men's side; featherweights don't hit with the same force as heavyweights. Because of that, there may be fewer knockdowns and less visible damage in many two-minute bouts.

That doesn't make these fights any less demanding to

judge. In fact, it makes them harder. When there isn't obvious damage to measure, judges have to lean even more heavily on the criteria: clean punching, effective aggression, defense, and ring generalship. Subtler signs, such as timing, accuracy, and control of distance, become the difference between winning and losing a round.

THE ILLUSION OF VOLUME

Two-minute rounds often feature higher punch volume, as fighters know they have less time to impress. That can create the illusion of dominance when, in reality, both are throwing, but few are landing clean. Judges have to cut through the noise. A busy fighter isn't necessarily a winning fighter. The scoring still comes down to quality, not quantity.

This is where being ringside matters. On TV, every punch can look like it lands. Ringside, you see the glancing blows, the shots picked off on the gloves, and the body language that reveals whether something was effective.

DAMAGE VS. EFFECTIVENESS

Another common pitfall is overvaluing visible damage. In some two-minute fights, there may not be much of it. That doesn't mean nothing's happening. A fighter controlling distance with the jab or slipping shots and countering cleanly may be winning without leaving marks. Judges must avoid the trap of thinking, "if nobody looks hurt, the round was even." It rarely is.

THE JUDGE'S RESPONSIBILITY

At the end of the day, a two-minute round is still a round. The criteria don't change: clean punching, effective aggression, ring generalship, and defense. What changes is the context. The judging job becomes less about waiting for a big moment and more about catching the smaller ones.

That requires discipline. You can't be a "highlight hunter," waiting for a fight to sort itself out. You have to track every sequence and weigh it against the full two minutes.

WHY IT MATTERS

Some might shrug and say a round is a round. But to the fighters, the stakes are huge. In a 10-round fight of two-minute rounds, there are only 20 minutes of action. That's one-third less time to make an impression compared to a 10-round fight of three-minute rounds. Every round matters more. Every close call by a judge carries more weight in shaping the outcome.

That's why two-minute rounds demand sharper judging. They are faster, more competitive, and less forgiving of error. They challenge judges to stay present, apply criteria consistently, and resist the easy narratives of volume or late flurries.

As the sport continues to evolve, the conversation about round length will continue. But until that changes, judges must recognize that two-minute rounds aren't just shorter; they're different. And they require us to bring our sharpest focus to the job.

SIDEBAR: WHY TWO-MINUTE ROUNDS?

The two-minute format in women's boxing traces back to early sanctioning guidelines in the 1990s when regulators sought to distinguish women's bouts from men's and, at the time, raised concerns about fighter safety. While those concerns were never backed by hard science, the shorter round length and lower maximum number of rounds, often 10 instead of 12, became the norm.

Today, many top women boxers argue for three-minute rounds, pointing out that the shorter format limits strategy, development, and even earning potential since a fight is literally one-third shorter. Organizations like the WBC have resisted the change, while others are open to experimenting.

For now, two-minute rounds remain standard in most jurisdictions. That makes it critical for judges to understand the unique dynamics of scoring them and to approach them with the same seriousness and precision as any other round.

THIRTEEN

The Hardest Rounds to Score

NOT ALL ROUNDS are created equal, and despite being armed with scoring criteria and years of experience, there are still some rounds that,if you can get them to admit it, give judges fits. We can all look at a round and see when one boxer hits the other boxer more often or harder or when they've obviously done more damage. Those aren't, or at least shouldn't be, the rounds that cause trouble.

On the other hand, there are rounds that call on judges to use, well, their judgment. As much as we'd like to declare that we can put a fine enough point on analyzing what's happening in the ring, some rounds will ultimately come down to the judges' thoughts, beliefs, and experience.

Let's take a look at some of those rounds and what you can do to determine a winner.

JABS VERSUS POWER SHOTS ROUNDS

This may be the most discussed, debated, and analyzed type of round to score, and for good reason. It asks the question: "How many jabs equal a power shot?"

There is no chart, calculus formula, or CompuBox equation to answer this question.

A judge must bring their knowledge of the sport and its mechanics to make a call. For me, that means analyzing the power in both the jabs and the power shots. The components of a good boxing punch include form, body weight behind the punch, where it connects, and the positioning of the boxer when they land the punch.

Good form is not just aesthetically pleasing—power is derived from form. When I studied Tae Kwon Do, our style used the analogy of an ocean wave, with the most powerful waves being the ones with the best form. A good jab has the body behind it; the boxer commits to it and is in position to land it. It snaps with the power of the arm and is thrown with intention. Jabs with the weight on the back leg, a foot turned ready to escape, and executed tentatively shouldn't be given as much credit when it comes to scoring.

Power shots, whether they are crosses, hooks, or uppercuts—should also be thrown with good body mechanics. That is, feet planted, weight moving forward, commitment to the punch, and executed with speed and force. To do this, the boxer must have crossed into the neutral zone, which means risking getting hit, and they must use the torque of shifting their body weight to throw the punch.

All of this happens in split seconds, and it is not absolute —boxers can meet some of these components but not all of them. This makes it very tough to evaluate in the moment, and it is why these rounds are challenging for judges.

In sum, judges should look for the positioning of the body weight, the commitment to enter the neutral zone to throw, and the shifting of body weight and torque of the body in executing the technique. Enter all that data into your evaluation of how many jabs equal a power shot and make your decision.

It isn't easy when fights are close.

THE INACTIVITY ROUND

At first glance, you might assume that these rounds happen when fighters are playing it safe, not being true warriors, and fighters who just aren't committed. That can be the case, but these rounds also occur with some of the very best boxers in the game.

In twelve-round fights between very evenly matched boxers, the early rounds, especially the first three, can be a feeling-out process. Both fighters can be cautious, evaluating distance, warming up, and concentrating on not getting caught early. They circle, paw jabs to measure distance and the opponent's reaction, and stay out of harm's way. Nothing lands with power, body shots are thrown without much behind them, and the fighters clinch to avoid danger.

Savvy boxers may pick up the pace close to the end of the round to win it. Sometimes this is referred to as "stealing the round," which is a term I don't like. A boxer either does more to win or not. If so little action has occurred throughout a round that one flurry wins it, then that's the other boxer's fault for being outworked.

In these feeling-out rounds, when a boxer picks up the energy with, say, 20 seconds to go and lands one jab, one decent body shot, or a flurry with even a little on it, that can be enough to win the round. That fighter gets the credit for winning a round 10-9.

Later in that bout, in a wickedly competitive 12th round, someone is going to win that round 10-9. Both rounds have the same weight and the exact same influence on the final score.

The strategy the judges must employ is to concentrate closely on those early rounds and evaluate the fine points of what is happening. It can be frustrating, and in championship fights, the stakes are very high. In fact, in every fight, the stakes are very high for those in the ring. Each round is its own separate entity. The scoring system is the scoring system, and all rounds count the same.

Keep that in mind when the final decision is announced.

SLOPPY ROUNDS

It is much easier for judges to evaluate experienced, skilled boxers than beginners. Experienced fighters use fundamentally sound techniques in the right way, and when those techniques land, evaluating the damage is pretty straightforward.

When boxers windmill punches, throw weird looping ninja shots, punch with no weight behind them, or any number of incorrect techniques, it is difficult to score. Certainly, unorthodox punches can do damage, but often they do not. When they land, a judge has to evaluate the technique as it was. You'll notice that four-round fights often have more disparate scores, and this is one of the reasons. The fighters are less experienced, and their technique has not been honed and refined.

Excessive clinching makes for unappealing boxing, and it can lead to difficult rounds to score. A punch isn't considered a scoring punch if it occurs while committing a foul, so holding and hitting shouldn't enter into a judge's scoring criteria. When two fighters clinch and lean on each other, throwing listless body shots back-and-forth for a whole round, it can be very difficult to sort out what is going on at a scoring level.

THE HIGH-ACTIVITY ROUND

When both fighters are aggressive, doing damage, and landing punches, it is also difficult. In this scenario, it is the volume of activity that makes it hard for a judge to keep evaluating. Sometimes a very busy round with a knockdown helps the judges by providing a clear delineation point. At that point, a judge may think they can relax, but what if five seconds later, the other fighter hits the canvas? Now the round is back to being unclear.

The answer is to judge the entire round just as the fighters have to work the entire round. That means following every engagement and keeping an ongoing tally in your head of who is winning. The Association of Boxing Commissions teaches that at any time when a round is stopped, a judge should know immediately what their score is. A judge must stay in the moment, in the action, and in scoring mode. It requires deep concentration.

Trust me, it is more relaxing to enjoy a fight from the couch, with a cold beverage, petting your basset hound, and listening to the TV commentators muse on the intricacies of the sweet science than it is to follow every millisecond, evaluating every muscle contraction and putting it into the scoring computer between your ears.

Good judging, when the rounds are tough, is hard work.

FOURTEEN

The 10-10 Round &
Why It Should Be Rare

EVERY ROUND in boxing is three minutes; 180 seconds of action, movement, and strategy. In those 180 seconds, it's a judge's job to analyze, compare, and decide who had the edge. Sometimes that's easy, and sometimes it's brutally difficult.

But it's always the job.

Still, there are situations that tempt a judge to call a round even. Here are three of the most common:

Scenario 1: The Back-and-Forth Round In a high-action round where both fighters are trading shots at a furious pace, and the damage appears more or less equal, a 10-10 score can feel like a safe call.

Some judges argue that scoring these rounds even allows the more definitive rounds to stand out clearly, helping identify the rightful winner on the final cards.

I'm not convinced. More importantly, that rationale doesn't align with the rules of judging. Even in a back-and-forth brawl, the judge is tasked with identifying who had the edge, however slight.

Scenario 2: The Low-Action Round Especially in the heavier divisions, rounds can devolve into lean-fests, clinch battles, or mutual agreements to conserve energy. Both fighters take a breather, and fans are left groaning.

Judges may be tempted to "toss" the round, score it even, and wait for something meaningful to happen in the next one.

Again, that's not judging. That's deferring. A round is a round, whether it's exciting or dreadful, and it still requires a winner.

Scenario 3: The Double Knockdown If both fighters hit the canvas in the same round, some may think the round cancels itself out.

It doesn't.

Knockdowns are important, but they're just one piece of the puzzle. Judges still have to weigh clean punching, ring control, defense, and effective aggression across the entire round.

Even in a wild exchange of knockdowns, someone usually did *just a little* more.

So, what should a judge do?

Simple: Pay attention. Concentrate. Focus.

It's not glamorous, but it's the job. If a fighter does even 1% more, lands one more clean shot, controls the ring slightly better, dictates pace just a hair longer, then they've done enough to win the round.

Let's be clear: even rounds are not illegal. But they should be extremely rare, used only when there is genuinely no way to separate the fighters using the four scoring criteria: clean punching, effective aggressiveness, ring generalship, and defense.

And that is almost never the case.

A judge's role is not to *watch* the fight; it's to *judge* it. If you can't find a winner after three full minutes of professional combat, you may not be paying close enough attention, or you may be afraid to take a stand.

Take the first Sugar Ray Leonard vs. Roberto Durán fight in 1980. One judge scored five rounds even. In a 15-round bout, that's a third of the fight left undecided. Some in the sport defend this approach, saying it allows only the most decisive rounds to count toward the final result.

But that logic doesn't hold up.

Judges aren't there to declare *only* the blowout rounds. They're there to score *every* round. And when they score too many 10-10s, they don't just abdicate their responsibility; they shift it to the other judges.

Close fights are often decided by razor-thin margins. Every point matters. Declining to make a call distorts the math and puts the outcome in someone else's hands.

Of course, there are rare moments; truly rare; when two fighters land cleanly and evenly, control space in equal measure, defend each other flawlessly, and no edge can be found.

Fine. Use 10-10 then. But if it becomes a habit, that judge probably isn't doing the job right.

Professional judging demands decisiveness, clarity, and accountability. If you want to call fights at the highest level, you have to be willing to make tough calls in tough rounds every single time.

In my 28 years of judging, covering over 625 fights and somewhere around 4,000 rounds, I've scored one round even.

I wish I hadn't.

FIFTEEN

Scoring the Slow Rounds

EVERY JUDGE KNOWS the adrenaline rounds, wild exchanges, knockdowns, and momentum swings. Scoring those can still be tricky, but at least the action gives you something to measure. It's the quiet rounds, the slow ones, the "nothing rounds," where your mental sharpness gets truly tested.

When both fighters are cautious, tentative, or maybe just tired, it's easy for everyone in the arena to check out. Fans groan. Announcers grasp for talking points. But for the judge, it's not time to relax—it's time to lock in even harder.

WHAT YOU'RE REALLY LOOKING FOR

In a slow round, your job is to find the slight edge. That means locking in on:

- Clean, effective punches — Maybe only five land the whole round. But did Fighter A land three and Fighter B only two? That's enough to win the round.

- Effective aggression — Is one fighter stepping forward, initiating exchanges, even if they're brief?

- Ring generalship — Who's dictating where the action happens? Who's forcing the other to react, even subtly?

- Defense — If punches are rare, you also evaluate who's making the other miss cleanly and staying composed.

It's not a round to throw away or call even out of frustration. There's almost always a winner, even in the quietest of rounds.

REAL-WORLD EXAMPLES

Take Floyd Mayweather Jr. vs. Manny Pacquiao (2015). In Round 1, and several others, you had two elite fighters barely engaging. But Mayweather's jab, distance control, and occasional clean right hand edged out Pacquiao's minimal output. Judges had to reward subtle success over simply coming forward.

Or consider Guillermo Rigondeaux vs. Nonito Donaire (2013), a masterclass in inactivity. Long sequences went by with just feints and footwork. Yet when Rigondeaux landed a sharp straight left or timed a counter, it had to be valued—despite the lack of volume.

Then there's Bernard Hopkins vs. Joe Calzaghe (2008), where both fighters had low connect rates. Hopkins landed the cleaner punches, but Calzaghe was busier. In rounds where little separated them, judges had to make razor-thin calls: cleaner vs. busier. That's not just preference—it's detailed observation.

Heavyweights weren't exempt either. In Wladimir Klitschko vs. Tyson Fury (2015), most rounds had single-digit connects. Fury's feints, angles, and occasional flicking jabs created just enough of an edge. Judges had to see past the boredom and into the nuances of movement and control.

Even fights with crowd noise and fanfare like Erislandy Lara vs. Canelo Alvarez (2014) featured these slow rounds. Lara's defense and movement versus Canelo's body attack forced judges to weigh clean evasion and ring generalship against low-volume aggression. The rounds were subtle—but far from even if you were watching carefully.

THE DANGER OF DISTRACTION

These are the rounds where even experienced judges can be tempted to mentally drift. It's a few seconds here, a glance at the crowd, or maybe the scoreboard. But that's when you miss the one clean shot or a tactical shift that should've tipped the round.

Discipline is staying fully engaged, even when the fighters aren't giving you much. You treat every second like it matters—because it does.

BOTTOM LINE

The slow round isn't a break; it's an assignment. It demands quiet attention, restraint, and experience. The dramatic rounds will get all the replays and tweets. But often, it's those subtle, early rounds—scored correctly—that decide the outcome.

And as a judge, those are the moments that show what kind of professional you are.

SIXTEEN

The Judge and the 10-8 Round

IN PROFESSIONAL BOXING, scoring a knockdown (usually) gets you an extra point and renders a 10-8 score for the round. That changes (usually) if both fighters score knockdowns. It can also change if a point is deducted by the referee for a foul.

That isn't the hard part to understand.

The hard part to understand is:

1. When can a single knockdown NOT result in an extra point?
2. When can an extra point be given when there is no knockdown?

Unfortunately, for those who like objective, solid, unvarying rules and guidelines, you're out of luck. There will be no shortage of explanations but very little to hang your hat on, point to, and be 100% certain of in this facet of judging.

Let's break it down.

THE "FLASH" KNOCKDOWN

Some TV commentators reference the "Flash" knockdown like it is a rulebook classification, a type or a category of the knockdown.

It isn't.

At least not when it comes to the scoring criteria.

If any part of a boxer's body touches the canvas other than the soles of their feet, it is considered a knockdown. Judges are supposed to award an extra point for a knockdown; though, officially, they aren't required to.

A knockdown should result in an extra point. Judges are trained to go with what the referee rules.

Much like Joe Friday on Dragnet (I realize I'm skewing a tad old here), judges are supposed to work on the facts. The question is—did the referee rule it a knockdown? If he or she did, it is a knockdown. Usually, that means an extra point.

It is generally considered that judges are not to overrule the referee.

"THE PILLAR TO POST" DOMINATION ROUND

Judges are trained to award an extra point in a non-knockdown round when one fighter totally dominates the other.

There's a problem with the semantics of this statement.

Define "dominate."

While you're at it, define "totally."

This is where the subjectivity of boxing gets in the way of the precision of scoring. Some of my colleagues will argue that they know it when they see it. They'll say it's when one boxer dominates the other "From Pillar to Post."

Despite the catchiness of the "Pillar to Post" alliteration and the "Knowing It When You See It" maxim, it doesn't exactly bring to boxing the same clarity that those computerized strike zones bring to baseball.

It still is subjective.

Consider:

Is it total domination if the fighter getting dominated lands a single jab?

Two jabs?

Three jabs?

What if the fighter getting beaten shows good defense and gets out of the way some of the time?

What if the fighter does that annoying smile thing and sticks out their tongue to show that they aren't hurt or...dominated? (Um, I'm trying to be funny here.)

It means it is subjective.

It means it is a matter of judgment.

This is where judging gets hard. Evaluating domination or what the ABC refers to as "Excessive Decisiveness" is in the eyes, brain, and interpretation of the judge.

Domination or "Excessive Decisiveness" should mean things like:

Did the ropes keep the opponent from hitting the canvas?

Were the punches damaging, causing staggering?

Was the fighter unable to mount any reasonable offense?

Did the losing boxer look like they were about to go down any second?

Once again...all of these have a great deal of subjectivity to them.

There is one thing that I am confident of: The use of the 10-8 non-knockdown rule should be used sparingly, carefully, and when it is totally warranted. It shouldn't be used in rounds that are just being won by one boxer.

Now, could there be other ways of scoring to fix this?

Probably.

We could use all of the numbers from one to ten. We could use half-points. You could do aggregate scoring.

The possibilities are almost endless.

However, and this is important, currently, we don't use any other system other than the 10-point must system. That's what we have, and to go rogue and try your own interpretation goes against the rules of the sport and will screw everything up.

Maybe changes could and even should be made, but until they are, judges need to follow the existing criteria.

SEVENTEEN

Split Decisions & Statistical Significance

WHY THE OUTLIER JUDGE ISN'T ALWAYS WRONG

A SPLIT DECISION in professional boxing can turn a great night into a controversial one. Two judges award the fight to one boxer, while a third goes the other way. Cue the Twitter outrage, the commentary desk criticism, and the inevitable question: "What fight was that judge watching?"

Despite how it is treated by the TV analysts or all the Twitter soldiers chiming in from their mom's basement, being the outlier doesn't automatically mean you got it wrong. Yet, the judge on the short side of the decision is often seen as being off. Some professionals even grade judges on how often they are in the majority.

Let's take a look at how probability and small sample sizes work and what it means when it comes to split decisions.

JUDGING WITH A SAMPLE SIZE OF THREE

There are three judges in a professional boxing match. In the world of statistics, that's what we call a very small sample size.

If two people see one thing and a third sees something else, does that automatically make the third person wrong? Not necessarily. In fact, with only three observers, a single dissenting opinion is expected to happen by chance from time to time. It's not a red flag unless it happens consistently over a large number of fights.

To truly determine whether a judge is a frequent outlier in a statistically significant way, you'd need many more observations; think 20, 30, or more judges all independently scoring the same fight. Then you could look at standard deviation. That's a statistic that tells you how much the judges' scores differ from one another. If most judges score the fight very similarly, say everyone has it 116–112 or 115–113, the standard deviation is small, indicating strong agreement. If scores are all over the place, such as 118–110, 115–113, or even for the other fighter, then the standard deviation is large, indicating wide disagreement and a fight that could have gone either way.

But with only three judges, you don't have that luxury.

CONSENSUS DOESN'T EQUAL CORRECTNESS

Consensus feels good. We like when everyone agrees, especially on something as intense and emotional as a close fight. But agreement isn't always truth.

Imagine 30 judges score a close fight, and 16 of them give it to Fighter A while 14 give it to Fighter B. There's a slight majority, but not an overwhelming one. That tells you it was a tough call. Now shrink that panel to just three. Two pick Fighter A, one picks Fighter B. Same proportion, same level of ambiguity, but suddenly the third judge is seen as the problem.

Statistically, that's not fair.

PERCEPTION AND POSITION MATTER

Judges sit at three different ringside positions, each with a unique view. What looks like a clean jab from one side might be partially blocked from another. A body shot that echoes through the arena might be muffled by crowd noise depending on where you sit. All of that affects scoring.

Add to that the psychological effects: confirmation bias (expecting a certain fighter to win), crowd influence, and the rapid pace of judging in real time with no replays. Even with rigorous training and consistent application of the scoring criteria, perception varies. That's why having multiple judges is a safeguard, not a guarantee of unanimity.

WHAT WOULD STATISTICAL SIGNIFICANCE LOOK LIKE?

To know whether there's a true consensus, not just chance, you need to look at something called confidence level. Statisticians often use a 95% confidence level, which means: *"If I repeated this test over and over, I'd expect to be correct 95 out of 100 times."*

In boxing terms, you'd want to be sure that the majority score for a fighter wasn't just random luck in a small sample; that it would likely hold up if you asked more judges.

In fact, you'd need about 385 judges scoring the same fight to be 95% sure the majority result wasn't just chance. That's how many scores it would take to say with confidence: *"Yes, this fighter was clearly seen as the winner by most experts."*

Here's an example: Say you want to know how most

judges would score a close round, one where both fighters had moments.

If you asked three judges, and two scored it for Fighter A, one for Fighter B, that doesn't tell you much; it could easily be random, especially in a close round.

But if you asked 385 judges, and 350 of them picked Fighter A, now you'd be much more confident—about 95% sure—that most experts really do see Fighter A as the winner.

Of course, boxing will never use hundreds of judges. But this underscores the point: with only three judges, even a 2–1 decision doesn't tell you who was right; only that the fight was close.

OUTLIERS ARE BUILT INTO THE SYSTEM

The three-judge model in boxing was created to protect against bias and bad decisions, not to guarantee perfect agreement. When a decision is split, it often just reflects the complexity of what unfolded in the ring.

Being the dissenting judge is part of the job. It doesn't mean you weren't paying attention or that you don't know what you're doing. It may simply mean that from your vantage point, with your training and your judgment, you saw it differently. And sometimes, in a close fight, that's not only okay; it's inevitable.

EIGHTEEN

Why Close Decisions Feel Like Robberies

THE PSYCHOLOGY OF CONSPIRACY IN BOXING

IN BOXING, nothing stirs outrage like a close decision that goes the "wrong" way, at least in the eyes of the public. A fighter who threw more punches but landed fewer loses. A crowd favorite gets outmaneuvered. The judges' scores don't match the TV analysts.

It happens almost every Saturday night. A great Pay-Per-View card gets "marred" by the controversy of a bad decision. Somebody seemed to land more, do more damage or simply outwork the other.

Next comes the accusations.

"This was a robbery."

"That judge was paid off."

"Boxing is corrupt — again."

Maybe it is from the TV analysts, maybe the reporters, certainly from social media and the accusations become accepted as truth.

Of course, there are bad decisions. Of course, judges are human and can get things wrong. The jump to conspiracy usually doesn't make any sense.

Never mind that the decision might have been correct or, at least, justifiable. At this point it isn't about the scorecard it is about how the human brain reacts to uncertainty, emotion and disappointment.

We see it in our culture every day. Social media breeds it. So, why would pro boxing be different.

Let's take a look at the dynamics of conspiracy theories and try to make sense of their impact on our sport.

Some of our culture's most popular conspiracy theories include the existence of Bigfoot, Alien visit coverups, Q-anon, assassination attempts—the list goes on and on. There's even a very prominent one brewing right now that I don't even want to name.

But why do they happen?

THE BRAIN WANTS CERTAINTY, NOT COMPLEXITY

When a bunch of people look up into the sky and see something they can't explain and are told it is an "Unidentified Flying Object" that breeds more questions than it does answers. When a crazed lone gunman takes out the most powerful man in the world from a book depository with a single bolt rifle shot--that countless marksmen can't reproduce—people believe it has to be something more.

So, when a boxing decision goes in a different direction than expected our brains starting working overtime to make sense of it. But the human mind doesn't like gray areas, especially in emotional situations. When a round is hard to call, and the result goes against expectation, fans don't think:

"That was close and could've gone either way."

Instead, they think:

"Something fishy is going on."

That's pattern seeking in action — the brain's attempt to connect dots that aren't actually related.

NARRATIVE BIAS: THE STORY MUST MAKE SENSE

Most fans come into a fight with a preferred narrative.

- A fighter is on a comeback.
- A champ is being avoided.
- An underdog is due for redemption.

When the decision disrupts that narrative, it doesn't just challenge a scorecard, it breaks the story. And the brain, desperate to preserve that story, fills the gap with blame.

That's narrative bias — when we favor emotionally satisfying explanations (like "he was robbed") over more nuanced, unsatisfying ones ("it was a close round"). Even better, we harken back to boxing's organized crime-controlled history and we apply it to what is in front of us. It makes more sense to our brains to believe in dark nefarious forces than to say, "Hmm, I guess it could've gone that way," or "Let me take another look at that round to see if I can see what the judge saw."

WHY LOSING CONTROL FEEDS BELIEF IN CORRUPTION

Fans can't control the outcome of a fight, especially when they've emotionally invested in a fighter. That lack of control creates psychological discomfort, and conspiracy theories become a coping mechanism.

"If the system is rigged, at least I understand why this happened."

That's more comforting than randomness. And it aligns

with existential motives — the brain's need to feel secure in a world that often isn't.

It is also more dramatic and exciting to believe in conspiracies than it is to look for a more rational explanation.

Every year the NFL puts out the Super Bowl logo before the start of the season. Conspiracy theorists say that it always holds the colors of the teams the NFL has preselected to be in the game that year. Never mind that there are countless years when it doesn't hold true or the fact that there are plenty of teams that share the same colors.

SOCIAL MEDIA IS A CONSPIRACY AMPLIFIER

A controversial decision used to get debated in gyms and bars. Now it's litigated in real time on Twitter, Facebook, and YouTube — where emotion trumps nuance, and engagement rewards outrage.

- A post that calmly breaks down a round might get 10 likes.
- A tweet that screams *"WORST ROBBERY EVER!!!"* gets 10,000.

Algorithms amplify emotion, not accuracy. And soon, fans aren't just reacting to the fight — they're reacting to each other's outrage. It becomes a feedback loop of fury.

Add in influencers and creators who monetize controversy, and you get a climate where even reasonable decisions get painted as scandal.

"THEY PAID OFF THE JUDGES!" – OR JUST A CLOSE FIGHT?

Let's take a step back.

- A fighter threw more punches, but landed fewer.
- He was busier, but the other was cleaner.
- All three judges had it close — 115-113, 114-114, 113-115.

That's not corruption. That's a high-level contest with subjective scoring.But to the fan whose fighter lost, the facts are secondary to the emotion of loss. The conspiracy theory serves as emotional protection, a way to turn vulnerability into certainty.

BOTTOM LINE: EVERY CLOSE FIGHT ISN'T A ROBBERY

Understanding the psychology behind conspiracy theories doesn't mean fans are irrational. It means they're human.

But if we want to keep trust in boxing — and respect for officials — we need to do better at recognizing the difference between:

- A close fight and a fix
- Disagreement and dishonesty
- Uncertainty and injustice

Judging isn't perfect. But more often than not, it's honest. And if we can see past our own biases, maybe we'll stop crying "robbery" every time a decision doesn't fit the story we brought to the ring.

NINETEEN

The Hidden Prejudices in Boxing Judging

JUDGES ARE SUPPOSED to score what happens inside the ropes using the four criteria: clean punches, effective aggression, defense, and ring generalship. That's it.

They're not supposed to factor in backstory, reputations, or emotions. But the truth is, no one comes into a fight with their mind completely erased.

Judges are human. And humans carry baggage.

THE GHOSTS OF KNOCKOUTS

Suppose a judge knows a fighter was knocked out in his last fight. Maybe they saw it on TV, or maybe they were even at ringside that night. That knowledge can sneak into the subconscious.

A guy who's been laid out before can look wobbly the moment he gets touched again, even if it's not much of a punch. That ghost knockout plays tricks on perception.

Take Meldrick Taylor. After Julio César Chávez stopped him dramatically in 1990, every subsequent fight was seen through that lens. Fans and judges alike were primed to see him as vulnerable. Past knockouts shouldn't color the present, but they whisper in your ear anyway.

They absolutely shouldn't. Judges are required to evaluate what's in front of them in the moment: nothing more, nothing less.

RECORDS THAT TELL STORIES

A fighter with a losing record enters the ring, and the story can seem pre-written. The journeyman with a ledger of 8–17, 17–55, or 2–27 steps in against a 14–0 prospect, and when the underdog lands, it doesn't always land on the scorecard the same way. His punches may be just as clean, but reputations carry invisible weight.

The assumption is that the B-sider was brought in to lose, and everyone knows it. But sometimes the B-side fighter forgets to read the script.

On smaller cards, mismatches happen more often. Fans rarely see the scramble promoters face when fighters don't make weight, fail physicals, or simply don't show up. Finding late replacements isn't easy, but plenty of fighters with bad records are willing to step in.

Judges know this. They see it all the time. But every fighter deserves an impartial evaluation, and sometimes the opponent has a night way above what was expected. Judges have to stay alert to that.

CORNERMEN AND STAR POWER

The corner matters more than we like to admit. When a Hall of Fame trainer is barking instructions, say Freddie Roach or Eddie Futch back in the day, it gives their fighter an aura of legitimacy. The other guy's cornerman may be a dedicated local coach who's forgotten more about boxing than most fans ever knew, but he doesn't have the spotlight. And that spotlight can cast a glow over every punch thrown.

If a thought like *"Gee, Freddie Roach is in the corner..."* crosses a judge's mind, they'd better double down on what they actually see, because cornermen don't throw punches.

You don't need to be an insider to spot who has money behind them. The entourage, the advisers, the layers of support—it's obvious. Meanwhile, the B-side fighter is standing with his brother in the corner and no one else. Sometimes that guy can really fight, and he deserves a fair shake.

TRUNKS, SHOES, AND PRESENTATION

It sounds silly, but it isn't. Flashy trunks, bright shoes, and a polished look draw the eye. Boxing is part sport, part theater, and judges don't watch in black and white.

When one fighter comes in with a custom robe and trunks, $300 shoes, and $400 Japanese gloves, while the other shows up in Walmart shorts, beat-up shoes, and a towel for a robe, those images can slip into a judge's consciousness.

Judges need to recognize how presentation can bias perception and then ignore it.

THE GEOGRAPHY FACTOR

Crowd noise is one of the loudest forms of bias. A Mexican fighter in Mexico City, an Irishman on St. Patrick's weekend in New York, or a Brit at the O2 Arena—every landed shot explodes with approval. And sometimes the crowd roars when nothing really landed.

Geography also comes into play with a fighter's hometown. Hear "Brooklyn," "Philadelphia," "Los Angeles," or "Detroit," and gyms like Gleason's, Frazier's, Wild Card, and Kronk come to mind. Hear "Canajoharie, New York," "Elkhart, Indiana," or "Pittstown, Pennsylvania," and nothing comes to mind.

Judges need to put those associations aside and score what's actually happening in the ring.

THE MENTAL LOAD OF NEUTRALITY

The biggest challenge in judging isn't scoring punches; it's resisting invisible forces. You've got to reset every round, every fight. The fighter with the glass jaw deserves a clean slate. The underdog's jab counts the same as the prospect's. Trunks and trainers don't throw punches. The crowd is noise, not evidence.

That's not easy in real time. You're making 36 separate mini-verdicts in a 12-round fight, each one decided in seconds but carrying consequences that can last a lifetime.

WHY IT MATTERS

When judges don't recognize their biases, fighters pay the price. Careers derail. Titles change hands unjustly. And fans lose trust. In a sport that already struggles for mainstream legitimacy, bad decisions driven by subconscious prejudice are deadly.

That's why the best judges I know spend as much energy on self-awareness as on eyesight. Before every fight, they remind themselves: clean slate. No history. No trunks. No trainers. Just the punches.

THE BOTTOM LINE

Judging isn't just about knowing the four scoring criteria. It's about knowing yourself.

The ghosts of past knockouts, the sway of records, the

glow of star trainers, the flash of trunks, and the roar of crowds—they're all trying to score the fight for you.

The job is to shut them out. Because in the end, every fighter deserves to be judged for what he does tonight, not for who he was yesterday.

Why Judges Disagree More in the Late Rounds

IF YOU STUDY enough fight scorecards, a pattern emerges: judges tend to disagree the most in the late rounds, particularly in championship fights that go the full 12. In rounds 10, 11, and 12, when fatigue sets in for the fighters and the stakes are highest, it's common to see wide variance in how each judge views the action.

This isn't just anecdotal. Statistical trends across dozens of high-level contests, whether they end in a unanimous, majority, or split decision, show judges are more likely to diverge in their scoring during the final three rounds than in earlier ones.

WHY DOES THIS HAPPEN?

1. Fighter Behavior Changes
2. Late rounds often see fighters alter their approach:

- The fighter ahead may become more defensive or
- cautious.
- The trailing fighter tends to press harder, increasing output, but not always
- effectiveness.

These shifts make the action more ambiguous. What one judge views as smart defense, another may see as coasting. A late rally might look like desperation to one judge and effective aggression to another.

1. Mental Fatigue
2. By the championship rounds, judges have been locked into a sustained concentration task for upward of 40 minutes. Even with training, prolonged attention demands can lead to:

- Decreased sensitivity to subtle differences in clean
- punching.
- Overreliance on visible aggression or crowd
- reaction.
- Greater variance in interpretation of close
- exchanges.

1. Narrative Influence
2. Judges are not immune to momentum. As the story of the fight unfolds, a subconscious sense of who "deserves" the round can creep in. In very close rounds, this narrative framing can tip the score one way or another, inconsistently across judges.
3. Pressure and Stakes
4. In a tight contest, the championship rounds can carry perceived extra weight. While all rounds are scored equally on paper, rounds 10 to 12 often feel decisive, leading judges to "lean in" to different cues when making their calls.

WHAT THE DATA SHOWS

To get a clearer sense of this pattern, I compiled round-by-round scorecard data from multiple high-profile 12-round fights across the past 20 years, using:

- BoxRec.com (official scorecards)
- CompuBox Round Breakdown Summaries
- Fan and media post-fight scorecard aggregators (such as Reddit's r/Boxing and BloodyElbow)

This analysis involved counting how often all three judges agreed on a round versus split decisions.

The results lined up with what many judges have suspected for years:

- Early rounds (1 to 4) tend to have higher agreement among judges (around 70 to 80%)
- .
- Mid-rounds (5 to 8) show moderate divergence (60 to 70%).
- Late rounds (9 to 12) have the highest rates of disagreement, with some rounds seeing all three judges score them
- differently.

RESEARCH SUPPORTS THE PATTERN

This growing divergence isn't random; it's the natural result of what's happening inside the ring and inside the judges' minds.

Recent studies help explain the dynamic. In "They Were

Robbed! Scoring by the Middlemost to Attenuate Biased Judging in Boxing," researchers Stuart Baumann and Carl Singleton point out that close fights tend to hinge on marginal rounds—exactly the kind of ambiguous late rounds where disagreement spikes. They propose a "majority-rounds rule" to reduce the impact of late-round divergence and bias.

Similarly, "Modeling Perceived and Real Bias in Combat Sports Scoring" highlights how perception shifts during a bout. Early impressions can "anchor" judges' expectations, while fatigue and crowd influence skew late-round evaluations. The result: what looks like an effective rally in round 12 may appear very different to each judge, especially in a tightly contested bout.

BOTTOM LINE

While every judge is trained to evaluate each round on its own merit, the conditions of the fight—both psychological and physical—make late-round consensus more elusive. That doesn't mean the system is broken, but it does highlight the importance of awareness, accountability, and perhaps even future innovations in judging protocols.

TWENTY-ONE

Perception & the Judge's Mind

THERE's a famous selective attention experiment created by University of Illinois psychology professor Dr. Daniel Simons. It has nothing to do with boxing, yet its implications may have everything to do with judging.

Take a look before you read any further:

https://www.youtube.com/watch?v=vJG698U2Mvo&t=45s

Your task: Count how many passes are made by the students wearing white shirts.

The correct answer is 15.

But did you see the gorilla?

Roughly 50% of people don't.

If you did see the gorilla, you probably find it hard to believe anyone could miss it. If you didn't, you're likely baffled at how something so obvious slipped by.

Dr. Simons's research shows there's no meaningful difference between "noticers" and "non-noticers" in terms of intelligence, focus, or concentration. The difference lies in what they're attending to. When your brain is locked onto one task, like counting passes, it may not register unexpected information.

It's not that you weren't paying attention. It's that you were paying attention too specifically.

Read This:

Paris in the

the spring

Did you catch both "the"s?

Most people don't. Our brains don't expect a duplicate, so they skip right over it. We take shortcuts, filling in what we *expect* to be there.

Now try this:

"Aoccdrnig to rscheearch at Cmabrigde Uinervtisy, it deosn't mttaer in waht oredr the ltteers in a wrod are, the olny iprmoetnt tihng is taht the frist and lsat ltteer be at the rghit pclae."

Despite the scrambled words, your brain easily decodes it. Why? Because it recognizes patterns and fills in gaps based on experience.

You might be thinking: "Neat stuff, Tom. Glad you went to college. But what does this have to do with judging pro boxing?"

Let's break it down.

SELECTIVE ATTENTION IN THE RING

What a judge chooses to focus on has a huge impact on what they perceive and what they miss. A judge might zero in on the jab battle, body work, or power punches.

Dr. Simons explains.

"If you knew nothing about the boxers and had only the perceptual information about what they did, then theoretically, you could be entirely objective."

But we don't judge in a vacuum. There's pre-fight knowledge, crowd noise, TV commentary, and bright lights, all of which influence attention and perception.

"Even without that context, two people can see the same thing differently. But differences in what you know and expect, like what a fighter is known for, also influence what you notice," Simons adds. "You could see the body puncher's body shots more clearly because you *expect* to see them. Your top-down beliefs will change how you focus your attention."

Officials often judge the same fighters multiple times. Familiarity creates patterns. And when focus narrows too much, like in the gorilla video, critical elements can be missed.

We've all seen rounds where clean jabs, sharp body shots, or effective ring generalship seem to go unrecognized. It may simply be because the judge wasn't attending to those actions.

EXPECTATION AND THE BIAS OF FAMILIARITY

That extra "the" you missed? That's your brain relying on expectation to process information. In boxing, this can be dangerous.

When an underdog is outboxing a heavy favorite, a judge may unconsciously "fill in" the action based on what they *expect* to see. That expectation can override what's actually happening.

"Going back to the gorilla," Simons says, "You don't see it because you're intently focused on something else. If a single fighter has your attention, you could miss what the other one is doing."

Before Buster Douglas knocked out Mike Tyson in the 10th round, only one judge had Douglas ahead, despite his dominance. Tyson's reputation as invincible may have influenced perception.

Now imagine if Hector Camacho had suddenly adopted a peek-a-boo stance and stalked his opponent like George Foreman. Would judges see what was actually happening or try to make it fit their existing expectations of Camacho's style?

RECOGNIZING PATTERNS AND GETTING TRAPPED BY THEM

We decoded the scrambled Cambridge sentence because our brains recognize patterns. The same happens in judging.

As noted, judges often score fights involving the same fighters multiple times. Over time, they begin to expect certain patterns: Fighter A is aggressive, Fighter B fades late, Fighter C lands the big shots.

"When a fighter is known for something," Simons says, "judges can wind up looking for that pattern and expecting to see it. While their attention is focused there, other action can be missed and not scored."

Judges follow the sport. They watch videos. They read press. But all that pre-fight context can cloud in-the-moment perception if not kept in check.

THE SOLUTION: AWARENESS AND SELF-REFLECTION

Cognitive science teaches us that human perception is not photographic. Memory is flawed. Attention is selective. We interpret what we see through the lens of experience.

That's not a weakness; it's human nature.

But as judges, we have to be aware of how perception can color what we see. We need to be present, to watch broadly, and to catch ourselves when our experience starts shaping what we *think* we saw.

"I wish I had an easy answer to make judging completely objective," Simons says. "The fact is, anything involving human perception and judgment will always have some subjectivity."

TWENTY-TWO

When the Greatest Isn't the Winner

HOW PERCEPTION AND
BIAS SHAPED ALI-NORTON

MUHAMMAD ALI and Ken Norton fought three times in the 1970s. The record shows Ali winning two out of three. But if you ask most ringside observers and even Ali himself, Norton may have deserved to sweep the series.

So how did the decisions go the other way?

As a boxing judge and a bit of a student of perception, I believe the answer lies not just in the punches thrown but in how the human brain processes what it sees. What follows isn't conspiracy; it is cognition. Here is how psychological principles likely played a role in how judges scored these fights.

CONFIRMATION BIAS: SEEING WHAT YOU EXPECT

Ali was a legend. His fights with Liston were iconic, and the dominance he showed against Patterson, Williams, and Terrell was a thing of boxing beauty.

Confirmation bias, the tendency to see what you expect to see, can kick in hard when you are watching someone with that kind of legacy.

Judges may have come in believing Ali was supposed to win. Ali was artful, and there is no doubt he drew the eye. Norton was tough and strong, but he was not the poetry in motion that Ali was.

The mind tends to register what it anticipates. In close rounds, that bias could have filled in the gaps in Ali's favor.

TOP-DOWN PERCEPTION: REPUTATION OVER REALITY

When a fighter has the aura of Ali, it affects how we interpret what is happening in the ring. A late-round flurry or slick head movement can seem like dominance even when the numbers tell a different story.

In their second fight, unofficial punch stats compiled from tape study showed:

- Ken Norton landed approximately 199 punches, including 114 jabs and 85 power shots.
- Ali landed around 160 punches, with 94 jabs and 66 power shots.

Yet Ali won by split decision. Even Ali later admitted he thought Norton deserved it.

Could it be that the judges were caught up in Ali's aura? Most of the world was; why would the judges have been any different?

THE HALO EFFECT: WHEN GREATNESS GLOWS

The halo effect causes us to view people we admire through a flattering lens. Ali's charisma and legacy may have influenced judges to overvalue his flashy moments and undervalue Norton's steady, technical work.

It is hard to overstate how much influence Ali had, and he played to it. The judges were human, and they were tasked with evaluating a man who had become larger than life.

RECENCY EFFECT: THE LAST THING YOU SEE

Ali was a master of closing the show, flurrying in the final 30 seconds of a round, igniting the crowd, and creating a memory that stuck. That is the recency effect at work: we tend to remember and give more weight to what happens last.

But a flashy finish does not always outweigh being outlanded for most of the round. Ali knew how to game the scoring system, and he knew exactly what to show the judges.

THE NUMBERS IN THE THIRD FIGHT

The most controversial decision came in their final bout at Yankee Stadium in 1976. According to retrospective punch stats from boxing analyst Lee Groves and others who reviewed the film:

- Norton: ~286 punches landed, 42% accuracy
- Ali: ~199 punches landed, 29% accuracy

Norton outlanded Ali in 10 of the 15 rounds. Yet all three judges gave the fight to Ali.

Even Ali said afterward:

"I honestly think he beat me."

Nearly 100 more punches landed by Norton. But with eyes fixed on The Greatest, perhaps the judges simply did not see him, almost like missing the gorilla in the famous selective attention video.

Social Influence: The Roar of the Crowd

The setting matters. When 30,000 fans at Yankee Stadium are chanting "Ali! Ali!" every time he twitches his shoulders, it gets in your head. Even trained judges can fall prey to social proof, the subtle psychological pull of the crowd.

The crowd, at least early on, was pro-Ali. Their reaction to his every movement could easily influence a judge's perception, even if only subconsciously.

And yet, by the end of the night, the Yankee Stadium crowd booed the decision.

THE VERDICT: PSYCHOLOGY ON THE SCORECARDS

This is not about corruption; it is about cognition. Human judgment is flawed, especially under pressure and the weight of expectation.

Ali vs. Norton was more than a trilogy. It was a case study in how perception and bias can affect outcomes.

Ken Norton may not have gotten the official nod in fights two and three. But if you go by the film, the numbers, and even Ali's own admission, he probably should have.

And in boxing, that is the kind of truth that does not always show up on the scorecard.

TWENTY-THREE

Should Boxing Judges Have Experience as Boxers?

IT'S A FAIR QUESTION: Should someone who judges a professional boxing match have ever stepped into the ring themselves?

I've been asked that before, sometimes by fighters, sometimes by fans, and sometimes by people who are flat-out angry about a decision. The assumption is: *If you've never boxed, how can you truly understand what's happening in there?*

It's a valid concern. But here's the truth: having been a boxer isn't necessary to be a good judge, but it absolutely helps.

UNDERSTANDING FROM THE OUTSIDE ISN'T EASY

Most people grow up playing at least one sport. Whether it's baseball, basketball, or football, we've thrown a pass, taken a shot, or stood in the batter's box. Even if we weren't elite athletes, we *felt* those sports from the inside. That gives fans and referees alike a basic reference point when watching or officiating.

But boxing is different.

The vast majority of people, including some boxing officials, have never laced up a glove, taken a body shot, or gasped for air in the middle of a sparring round. The ring is a foreign world. Judging from the outside can feel like watching something through glass.

So, while it's not a prerequisite, having been in there, even just in the amateurs or in the gym, gives a judge insight that's hard to teach.

WHAT RING EXPERIENCE ADDS

I'm not saying you have to have been a pro. You don't need a championship belt to score a fight correctly. But if you've ever sparred a few rounds or trained seriously, you gain a better understanding of some key things:

- **When a fighter is tired** – You notice the little tells: the shoulders sagging, the feet getting stuck, the body language slipping.
- **When a punch hurts** – Not just from facial expressions, but from the way a fighter reacts or doesn't react.
- **When a punch looks good but doesn't land clean** – You've been hit with glancing shots, and you've landed them. You know the difference.
- **When someone's surviving vs. controlling** – It's subtle, but lived experience makes that easier to spot.

You also develop a deep respect for what fighters go through: the pain, the risk, the exhaustion, and the courage it takes just to show up. That respect can help keep a judge sharp, humble, and focused on fairness.

CAN FIGHT EXPERIENCE GET IN THE WAY?

Former pro fighters are an interesting lot. They've fought literally thousands of rounds in the gym, the amateurs, and the pros. That's a wealth of experience, but the gym culture is different from the arena and the scoring culture.

Some seasoned fighters can watch a gym war and see one of the fighters get hit way more than the other and come away believing the fighter throwing less won the "gym" round.

A veteran fighter will sometimes take shots while they are working on something. They may counter less often but sharper and harder. In the gym, the knowing eyes know who is getting the better of the round.

On fight night, under the bright lights, sometimes better fighters revert to gym habits. Experienced fighters may view what's going on through a gym lens, not an official scoring lens, because they know who is doing more complex or significant work.

Sometimes that runs contrary to scoring.

Former fighters have to put on another hat while scoring versus when they watch gym work because they are two different things.

WHAT CAN JUDGES WITHOUT RING EXPERIENCE DO

Let me be clear: some of the very best judges have never boxed, and they understand all the intricacies of the sport and scoring.

Taking some boxing lessons or classes might improve judging if a judge doesn't have the experience. Knowing how a proper punch is thrown, the body mechanics, and the shifting of body weight can help a judge understand what they are watching while scoring. Balance, footwork, and where power comes from can all help a judge do their job.

No need for a broken nose or a cauliflower ear, but understanding and experiencing the mechanics of good boxing can really help.

SKILL OVER EXPERIENCE

That said, I've worked with judges who've never boxed a day in their lives, and they're excellent. They study the craft, stay objective, and follow the criteria. They know the difference between scoring clean punches and being swayed by the crowd. They don't need to have fought to see the fight.

The key is discipline, focus, and judgment, not gym wars.

BOTTOM LINE

Boxing judging is not about who's tougher or who's been in the ring. It's about scoring each round with consistency and clarity, based on what actually happens.

But if you have boxed, even just trained seriously, you bring something extra: a better eye for what matters, a deeper respect for the fighters, and a little more empathy for what it takes to leave it all in the ring.

That doesn't make you a better judge by default, but it doesn't hurt either.

TWENTY-FOUR

How to Improve Judging with Deliberate Practice

DR. ANDERS ERICSSON's bestselling book *Peak: Secrets From the New Science of Expertise* is based on years of rigorous academic study on becoming the very best at anything. It lays out a clear blueprint for mastery, found in what Ericsson calls "deliberate practice." Mastery is available to all of us if we are willing to apply these studied principles.

Ericsson has spent his life examining the best violinists, ballet prodigies, free-throw shooters, and gymnasts. He has determined that, without exception, expertise comes not from predisposed talent but from years of focused, deliberate practice.

But can you become a better boxing judge by applying the principles of deliberate practice?

DEFINING DELIBERATE PRACTICE

It is important to distinguish between practice, purposeful practice, and actual deliberate practice. Practice, loosely defined, could be any activity related to one's goal. Basketball players may shoot around, baseball players may visit the batting cage, and quarterbacks can play catch with their receivers. Similarly, judges can work more fights, study televised bouts, or dig deep into YouTube.

Purposeful practice, however, is a particular type of practice that involves focusing intently on the activity and pushing beyond one's comfort zone. For example, it might mean paying close attention to body movements, positioning, and decision-making. It could involve focused videotape study rather than casually watching fight films.

Deliberate practice goes a step further. It has the intensity of purposeful practice, intense focus, and work beyond the comfort zone, but it also adds feedback from an expert coach. That coach provides continual feedback, usually on one facet of practice at a time, resulting in repetitions until the skill is performed correctly. The best coaches are either exceptional performers themselves or have worked with the best and understand what it takes to excel. It is informed practice guided by the best performers' accomplishments and an understanding of what these experts do to excel.

Perhaps the most important component of deliberate practice is the use of feedback and modification from a monitoring expert. Improvement involves constant tinkering and adapting as mistakes are made, reviewed, and corrected through repeated activity.

THE CHALLENGES OF JUDGING PROFESSIONAL BOXING

Sure, you're thinking, this is great, and when I want to take up the violin or set out for gold on the pommel horse in the 2028 Olympic Games, I'll dive right into deliberate practice. Right now, though, I want to be the best possible and most accurate boxing judge.

Several high-level professional sports come very close to drilling their officials in deliberate practice. An article published in the *Journal of Psychology of Sport and Exercise* rigorously examined the use of deliberate practice with rugby officials. Using video recordings of challenging calls, referees were asked to make a ruling. The video was slowed down, and participants received feedback on their calls from experienced expert judges. Later, the videos' speed was increased, and participants were asked to make similarly challenging calls. The participants all showed significant improvement after this training in their on-field experience.

The *Journal of Psychology of Sport and Exercise* has reported similar results in studies involving international soccer.

In the United States, the Professional Referee Organization, which oversees all levels of professional soccer, has developed an extensive internet-based video library. As often as weekly, referees participate in online training sessions, challenging them to make proper calls in difficult situations. The videos are presented, sometimes in slow motion, and officials are asked to make the correct call. Then, they receive feedback on their decision-making process. This type of continual practice helps officials develop the mental representations needed to improve on-field performance.

SUBJECTIVE JUDGING IN ATHLETICS

At first glance, comparing the brutal sport of professional boxing and the beauty of rhythmic gymnastics seems ludicrous. Yet, the mental processing involved in both activities is remarkably similar. Unlike on-field officiating, which relies on clear rules and regulations that can be objectively observed and processed, judges must rely on their own experience, knowledge, and expertise.

HOW CAN THAT BE IMPROVED?

A study published in the *Journal of Psychology of Sport and Exercise* examined the "Think Aloud" method of training. Expert judges watched videos of gymnasts' performances and narrated their thinking process regarding scoring. The results showed promising improvements in judges' ability to note complex movements such as loss of balance, bending of arms and knees, and foot positioning—all important components of scoring.

Wouldn't the observation of two boxers competing in clean punching, effective aggressiveness, ring generalship/control, and defense involve a similar mental process?

DELIBERATE PRACTICE FOR PROFESSIONAL BOXING JUDGES

In an interview with Dr. Ericsson on the topic of improvement in boxing judging, he suggested the following steps:

1. Choose challenging rounds of professional fights. Have experienced, respected judges and novices narrate rounds using the Think Aloud method.
2. Show the round in slow motion, with judges narrating in detail the ebb and flow of the round regarding scoring criteria.
3. Focus Think Aloud narration on scoring criteria, particularly clean punching.
4. Provide constructive feedback to less experienced judges where necessary.

5. Repeat training on different videos and
    continually provide feedback.

During the *Think Aloud* narration, judges can comment on actions like:

1. The body weight being behind the force of a
    punch.
2. Whether boxers are committing through the
    neutral zone to get full force of their power.
3. Whether a punch was in the proper form and
    therefore having maximum power.
4. Did punches land full or were they blocked or
    partially blocked?
5. Is a fighter effectively moving forward?
6. Is a fighter's aggression effective or is it merely
    activity?
7. Is a fighter's balance behind her punches
    indicating maximum power?

A PRACTICAL SYSTEM FOR DELIBERATE PRACTICE

Thanks to today's technology and the internet, introducing such continuous training would not be difficult. Much like soccer's Professional Referee Organization, a bank of rounds could be continually updated and narrated by experienced judges who could score the slow-motion rounds. These videos could be circulated to other officials, with constructive feedback provided via email or platforms like Skype—even in real time.

Experienced judges could stay sharp between bouts by

practicing and receiving feedback from peers and more seasoned officials. By making thought processes transparent, judges could form clearer mental representations of proper scoring, potentially leading to greater consistency among professional judges.

TWENTY-FIVE

How to Become a Professional Boxing Judge

EVERY SO OFTEN, someone leans over at ringside or catches me between bouts and asks some version of the same question:

"How do you become a boxing judge?"

It's a fair question. From the outside, judging can look mysterious; three officials sitting quietly at ringside, pencils moving, scorecards turning in. There's no obvious ladder, no draft, no combine. Unlike fighters, judges don't enter the sport through bright lights and televised debuts.

The truth is both simpler and more demanding than most people expect.

There is a path. But it requires patience, credibility, and a deep understanding of the sport that goes far beyond watching fights on television.

Let's walk through what the journey actually looks like.

START WITH THE SPORT ITSELF

Before anything else, a prospective judge needs immersion in boxing.

Not casual fandom. Not highlight watching. Real exposure.

You need to understand:

- how rounds develop

- how styles interact
- what effective punching actually looks like
- how defense can subtly win exchanges
- how momentum shifts inside three minutes

The best officials are students of the sport long before they ever hold a scorecard. Many come from backgrounds in officiating, coaching, refereeing, journalism, or serious amateur study of the game.

If you're serious about judging, start by watching fights with intention. Score them and compare your cards to official results. More importantly, compare your reasoning.

This is not about being right every time. It's about learning to see clearly.

LEARN THE CRITERIA PRECISELY

Every professional judge must master the four scoring criteria:

- clean punching
- effective aggression
- ring generalship
- defense

Knowing the words is easy. Applying them in real time is the craft.

A common mistake aspiring judges make is overvaluing one element, usually aggression or punch volume, without properly weighing effectiveness. Another is being overly influenced by crowd reaction or commentary narratives.

Serious candidates study the criteria until they become second nature. When a round ends, the trained judge should already know, not guess, which fighter most effectively met the standard.

This kind of clarity only comes from repetition and disciplined observation.

GET INVOLVED AT THE LOCAL LEVEL

Professional judging rarely begins at the professional level.
Most officials build experience through:

- amateur boxing programs
- local officiating assignments
- supervised judging opportunities
- training seminars and clinics

These environments are where fundamentals are sharpened. They are also where reputations begin to form.

One reality of this profession is that trust matters enormously. Assigning authorities look for individuals who demonstrate:

- consistency
- professionalism
- emotional composure
- attention to detail
- the ability to work within established protocols

Showing up prepared, respectful, and reliable matters as much as technical knowledge.

SEEK OUT FORMAL TRAINING

Quality training is essential.

Serious aspiring judges should attend recognized officiating clinics and educational programs whenever possible. These settings provide:

- standardized instruction
- supervised scoring practice
- feedback from experienced officials
- exposure to common judging pitfalls
- networking within the officiating community

This is where many candidates first realize how different real-time judging is from scoring fights on the couch.

Under structured evaluation, small habits become visible; hesitations, overreactions to crowd noise, inconsistent use of criteria. Good training helps smooth those edges early.

DEVELOP THE PROFESSIONAL MINDSET

Judging is not just technical. It is psychological.

A professional judge must cultivate:

Composure under pressure

Close fights create emotional environments. The judge must remain steady regardless of crowd reaction, corner behavior, or broadcast narrative.

Independence of thought

Three competent judges can reasonably disagree on close rounds. The goal is not consensus. The goal is honest, criteria-based scoring.

Focus and stamina

Twelve rounds of concentrated observation is mentally demanding. There are no replays. No rewinds. No second looks.

Humility

Even experienced judges continue to study the craft. The sport evolves; styles change.

Build a Reputation for Consistency

Advancement in judging rarely comes from one impressive performance. It comes from steady reliability over time.

Assignors and supervisors tend to notice officials who:

- turn in clean, organized scorecards
- demonstrate round-to-round consistency
- avoid dramatic swings without clear cause
- show professionalism before, during, and after events

In this profession, reputation travels quietly but quickly.

Do the work well, repeatedly, and opportunities tend to follow.

Understand the Time Commitment

This is not an overnight journey.

Becoming a trusted professional judge often takes years of:

- study
- supervised experience
- travel
- ongoing evaluation

Even after reaching the professional ranks, learning

never stops. The best judges I've known, officials with decades in the sport, still review fights, attend training, and discuss close rounds with colleagues.

If you're looking for quick access to ringside seats, this probably isn't the right path.

If you're drawn to the craft itself, you're in the right neighborhood.

COMMON MISCONCEPTIONS

Let's clear up a few myths.

Myth: Watching a lot of boxing is enough.It isn't. Intentional study and formal training matter.

Myth: Judges should always agree.Close rounds invite reasonable disagreement.

Myth: Crowd reaction tells the story of the round.It often tells you who landed the flashiest punch, not who won the round.

Myth: The job gets easier with experience.In some ways, it does. In others, you simply become more aware of the responsibility.

FINAL THOUGHTS

Judging professional boxing is demanding, often thankless work. It requires concentration, integrity, and a willingness to make firm decisions in real time while the world second-guesses them in slow motion.

But for those who truly love the sport,who appreciate its subtleties and respect its structure, it is also deeply rewarding.

If you choose to pursue this path, be patient. Be

studious. Be professional long before anyone hands you a professional assignment.

And remember:

The goal is not to be perfect.

The goal is to be consistently, honestly right for the right reasons.

TWENTY-SIX

The Future of Boxing Judging

EVERY FEW YEARS, usually after a high-profile controversy, the same question resurfaces:

Is it time to fix boxing judging?

It's an understandable reaction. Close fights stir emotion. Disputed decisions generate headlines. And in an era of instant replay, advanced analytics, and high-definition everything, the idea of three human beings making irreversible decisions in real time can feel, to some observers, almost antiquated.

But before we rush toward technological salvation, it's worth remembering something important:

Judging professional boxing is not broken in the way many critics believe.

It is imperfect. It is human. It is occasionally frustrating. But it is also rooted in a century of practical experience evaluating one of the most fluid and subjective sports in existence.

The future of judging will likely involve evolution, not revolution. The real challenge is separating improvements that genuinely enhance fairness from changes that merely create the illusion of precision.

Let's examine where the sport may be headed.

TECHNOLOGY: PROMISE AND PITFALLS

Technology is the most discussed potential disruptor in boxing judging. From punch-tracking systems to ringside monitors to expanded replay review, the tools available today are far more sophisticated than those of even twenty years ago.

Used wisely, technology can help. Used poorly, it can mislead.

THE POTENTIAL ADVANTAGES

1. Enhanced transparency

One of the greatest benefits technology offers is visibility. When fans can see punch totals, alternative angles, and real-time data, the process feels less opaque. Even when people disagree with a decision, understanding the information available to officials can increase trust in the system.

2. Training support for judges

Video libraries, digital scoring simulations, and post-fight analytics are extremely valuable educational tools. Modern judges can review their own work with a level of detail that earlier generations never had. This has already improved consistency in many officiating circles.

3. Supplemental, not primary, data

When used appropriately, tools like punch statistics can help commissions and trainers identify trends over time. They can highlight activity patterns, defensive success rates, and stylistic tendencies that enrich the broader understanding of the sport.

Notice the key word: supplemental.

Where technology becomes dangerous is when it begins to masquerade as definitive.

THE RISKS AND LIMITATIONS

1. The illusion of precision

Boxing is not baseball. It is not tennis. It is not a sport easily reduced to clean, objective counts.

Automated punch systems struggle with:

- partially blocked shots
- glancing blows
- body shots obscured by angle
- punches that land but lack meaningful effect
- punches that miss but draw crowd reaction

Numbers can look authoritative while still missing the essence of effective punching.

2. Overreliance on monitors

Some have proposed that judges should watch fights primarily on screens rather than directly from ringside. At first glance, this sounds modern and efficient. In practice, it introduces its own problems.

Monitors flatten depth perception. They can miss the physical impact of punches. They often lag slightly behind real time. And perhaps most importantly, they remove the judge from the physical immediacy of the bout, the very thing the scoring criteria were designed around.

There is a reason experienced officials value the live vantage point.

3. Replay creep

Expanded replay in boxing sounds appealing, but it raises difficult questions:

- What moments are reviewable?
- Who initiates the review?
- How long can reviews last before disrupting the flow of the bout?
- Does selective replay create more controversy rather than less?

Replay works best in sports with discrete, stoppable events. Boxing is continuous and fluid. Introducing too much replay risks solving one problem while creating several new ones.

THE PHYSICAL PLACEMENT OF JUDGES

One of the quieter but important conversations in the sport involves where judges should physically sit.

Traditionally, judges are positioned ringside at three different sides of the ring. This system has endured because it acknowledges a basic truth: boxing looks different from different angles.

ADVANTAGES OF THE TRADITIONAL RINGSIDE POSITION

- Judges experience the fight in real time
- Depth and impact are easier to assess live
- Multiple viewing angles create healthy scoring diversity
- Officials remain fully immersed in the bout

The current model is not accidental. It evolved through decades of practical experience.

POTENTIAL DRAWBACKS

- Sightlines can occasionally be obstructed
- Ring posts and referee positioning can interfere
- Crowd proximity can introduce environmental noise
- Different angles can produce different impressions

Critics sometimes view these differences as flaws. In reality, some degree of variation is inevitable in a sport this dynamic.

HYBRID APPROACHES: A POSSIBLE MIDDLE GROUND

The most promising future may not be all technology or all tradition, but thoughtful hybrid models.

Possible evolutions include:

- maintaining ringside judges while providing limited monitor support between rounds
- enhanced positioning guidelines to minimize blocked sightlines
- improved judge rotation and assignment diversity
- expanded post-fight review for training purposes, not decision
- reversal

The key principle should be this:

Technology should assist trained human judgment, not attempt to replace it.

THE SELECTION AND DEVELOPMENT OF JUDGES

If there is one area where the sport can continue to improve meaningfully, it is in the identification, training, and development of officials.

The future of judging depends less on machines and more on people.

WHAT MATTERS MOST

Consistency of training

Standardized education across jurisdictions helps ensure that scoring criteria are applied uniformly.

Ongoing evaluation

The best officials welcome feedback and periodic review. Judging is a craft that benefits from continual refinement.

Professional temperament

Composure, independence, and focus remain irreplaceable qualities. No technology substitutes for emotional steadiness under pressure.

Diverse experience pathways

Encouraging qualified candidates from varied backgrounds strengthens the officiating pool and reduces insularity.

The Evolution of Boxing Itself

Another often overlooked factor is that judging does not exist in a vacuum. It evolves alongside the sport.

Modern boxing features:

- more mobile fighters
- more emphasis on defensive movement
- more tactical pacing
- greater stylistic diversity

These changes make some fights inherently more difficult to score than the toe-to-toe battles of earlier eras. As styles continue to evolve, judge education must evolve with them.

The future judge must be fluent in both pressure fighting and high-level movement boxing and everything in between.

WHAT SHOULD NOT CHANGE

In all the discussion about reform, modernization, and innovation, it is worth stating clearly what still works.

The core principles of professional boxing judging remain sound:

- real-time human evaluation
- application of the four scoring criteria
- round-by-round assessment
- independent scorecards from multiple officials

These elements have endured because they reflect the fundamentally subjective nature of the sport.

The goal should not be to eliminate human judgment.

The goal should be to make human judgment as informed, trained, and consistent as possible.

FINAL THOUGHTS

The future of boxing judging will almost certainly include more data, more video support, and more public scrutiny than ever before. That is neither inherently good nor inherently bad. It simply reflects the broader technological moment in which the sport exists.

Progress in judging will come not from chasing perfect objectivity, an unrealistic goal in a sport as fluid as boxing, but from thoughtful refinement of the systems already in place.

Better training. Smarter use of technology. Careful judge selection. Ongoing education.

Get those right, and the scorecards will continue to reflect what they are meant to reflect:

Three trained observers doing their best, in real time, to fairly evaluate one of the most complex sports in the world.

And despite what the loudest voices sometimes claim, that system, properly supported, still works remarkably well.

TWENTY-SEVEN

Boxing Is for Everyone

OVER THE YEARS, I've learned that boxing gyms come in all shapes and sizes and that the stereotypes and preconceived notions about what they are like simply don't fit.

The general public often sees our sport as too violent, only for the young, the male, the city toughs, and for elite athletes—certainly not for anyone with a disability.

I understand where those perceptions come from. Boxing, at the professional level, is a demanding and sometimes brutal sport. But over the years—especially through my work in training and human services—I've come to believe something strongly:

Boxing, properly taught and thoughtfully adapted, is one of the most inclusive athletic activities we have.

It is not just for fighters. Boxing is for everyone.

BEYOND THE PRIZEFIGHT

When most people think of boxing, they picture the bright lights: championship bouts, dramatic knockouts, and elite athletes at the peak of physical condition.

But step inside a well-run community boxing gym, and you see something very different.

You'll see kids building confidence and a sense of community. You'll see adults getting in shape and learning how to throw a punch. You'll see folks with Parkinson's working on balance and determination, and you'll see people of all abilities working hard and having fun.

Boxing training, especially non-contact boxing, is uniquely adaptable. The core elements can be scaled up or down, and that applies to footwork, heavy bag rhythm, mitt work, and coordination drills.

You don't need to spar to benefit from boxing. In fact, many of the most powerful programs never involve contact at all.

WHY BOXING WORKS SO WELL

There's a reason boxing-based fitness has expanded far beyond the competitive ranks.

Boxing naturally develops bilateral coordination, cross-body movement, balance and posture, reaction time, cardiovascular endurance, and, just as importantly, focus.

The structure of rounds—work, rest, repeat—is neurologically friendly. The combination of rhythm and variation keeps participants engaged. And the immediate feedback of hitting a bag or mitt provides motivation that traditional exercise sometimes lacks.

In my experience, boxing meets people where they are and then gently challenges them to do a little more.

LEARNING FROM PARKINSON'S PROGRAMS

One of the clearest examples of boxing's broader impact comes from programs developed for people living with Parkinson's disease.

Across the country, non-contact boxing fitness programs have demonstrated encouraging results in helping participants improve balance, coordination, strength, and overall quality of life. Structured boxing workouts move the body through multiple planes while constantly varying the routine—exactly the kind of stimulus many neurological conditions respond well to.

Equally important, these programs build community. Participants train together, support one another, and regain a sense of agency that chronic illness often erodes.

In Schenectady, the Ring of Hope Boxing Club offers free Rock Steady classes for individuals living with Parkinson's, focusing on balance, strength, speed, and coordination in a supportive group environment.

What stands out is not just the physical progress; it's the confidence that returns.

That lesson carries over powerfully into other populations.

THE BIRTH OF UNDISPUTED CHAMPIONS

My own work in boxing grew naturally out of my background in human services and my lifelong involvement in boxing.

Through a partnership with Wildwood Programs and Ring of Hope, we launched **Undisputed Champions**, an adaptive boxing program for individuals with autism and other developmental disabilities.

From the beginning, the goal was simple: We wanted to create a structured, respectful boxing environment where every participant could succeed regardless of their ability. From the beginning, Colonie Police Sergeant Javy Martinez, Adapted Physical Education Teacher Rachel McDonough, and I set out to do a program that wasn't watered down, softened, or patronizing. We wanted hard work and boxing fundamentals thoughtfully adapted.

WHAT THE PROGRAM LOOKS LIKE

A typical Undisputed Champions session includes structured warm-ups, stance and guard work, heavy bag rounds, focus mitt drills, simple defensive movement, conditioning games, and, just as important, predictable routines.

For many participants on the autism spectrum, predictability is crucial. So is clarity of instruction. So is pacing.

We use visual modeling,consistent round structure, clear start/stop cues, graduated skill progressions, and plenty of positive reinforcement.

What we do not do is assume limitation.

Participants are expected to work—to focus, to improve, and time after time, they do.

WHAT WE SEE IN THE GYM

The changes are often striking.

Participants who begin cautiously—sometimes hesitant even to approach the bag—start to throw sharper punches,maintain stance longer, tolerate longer work intervals, follow multi-step instructions, and engage more comfortably with peers.

Parents and caregivers frequently report improvements that extend beyond the gym: better focus, improved regulation, increased confidence, and willingness to try new activities.

Is boxing a cure-all? Of course not.

But in the right environment, it is a remarkably powerful tool.

THE POWER OF THE RIGHT ENVIRONMENT

Programs like those at Ring of Hope succeed because they are intentionally holistic. The club's mission has long emphasized building physical well-being alongside emotional health, discipline, and community support.

That philosophy matters.

Adaptive boxing only works when the culture of the gym supports patience, safety, dignity, and genuine inclusion.

You cannot fake that environment. Participants, especially those with developmental differences, read authenticity quickly.

When the culture is right, progress follows.

ADDRESSING THE SAFETY QUESTION

Whenever adaptive boxing comes up, someone inevitably asks:

Is it safe?

The answer depends entirely on how the program is structured.

Proper adaptive boxing programs are non-contact, emphasize controlled technique, use appropriate supervision ratios, modify intensity individually, and maintain clear behavioral expectations.

In that format, boxing training is no more inherently risky than many other structured fitness activities and often more engaging.

The key is thoughtful design and trained leadership.

BOXING'S EXPANDING FUTURE

If there is one trend I am confident about, it is that boxing fitness will continue expanding into therapeutic and adaptive spaces.

We are already seeing growth in programs for Parkinson's disease, autism spectrum participants, older adults, trauma recovery populations, and general wellness communities.

This does not dilute the sport.

If anything, it strengthens boxing's relevance in the modern world.

Because at its core, boxing has always been about disciplined movement, controlled effort, and personal challenge. Those principles translate remarkably well when applied with care.

FINAL THOUGHTS

I have spent much of my career judging professional fights at the highest levels of the sport. I respect the elite side of boxing deeply.

But some of the most meaningful moments I've experienced in this sport haven't happened under bright lights.

They've happened in community gyms, in adaptive sessions, in the moment when a participant who wasn't sure they could do it... does.

Boxing, when taught responsibly, is not just for contenders and champions.

It is for anyone willing to step up to the bag, focus on the next round, and discover what they're capable of.

That's a future for the sport worth investing in.

About the Author

TOM SCHRECK is a boxing judge and author of Amazon's #1 hard-boiled mystery series, The Duffy Mysteries. He is a columnist with Westchester Magazine and a frequent contributor to Crimespree Magazine, Referee, and other publications.

He counts Robert B. Parker, John D. MacDonald, JA Konrath, Reed Farrel Coleman, Ken Bruen, and Michael Connelly among his favorite crime fiction authors. You can dive into his fiction catalog by reading his Duffy Mystery series and Trace Curran Thriller series.

Follow Tom and Subscribe to updates at
TomSchreck.com

Books By Tom Schreck

The Duffy Dombrowski Mysteries

On the Ropes

TKO

Out Cold

The Vegas Knockout

The Ten Count

The Comeback

The Shuffle

The Real Deal

The Split Decision

Getting Dunn

Redeeming Trace

The Second Burning